シリーズ
人と風と景と
Seen Scenes Series

吉村元男の「景」と「いのちの詩」

Landscape and the Poetry of Life
YOSHIMURA Motoo

京都通信社
K.T.P. Books
Kyoto Tsushinsha Press

もくじ

中くらいの自然 ……………………………………… 3
森に囲まれた平坦で広い空地 ……………………… 4
いのちを育み、つなぐ水辺と水面 ………………… 8
奇跡の沼が、いのちをつなぐ ……………………… 10
天と地をつなぐ垂直の庭園 ………………………… 12
超高層建築の下の新しい伝説 ……………………… 14
つながり、むすびあい、溶け込む風景 …………… 16

■白鳥庭園 …………………………………………… 18
せめぎあう水辺／水面に浮かぶ／
汐入の庭に込められた宇宙

■大阪府立国際会議場 葦原の庭 ………………… 24
暗闇を引き裂く／合理の葦の森

■新梅田シティ 中自然の森 ……………………… 30
都市の始まりの水／抱かれた地球／ビルの断層／
九条の水滝／滝の向こうから／石畳の下の饗宴／
四角・丸・三角／逆流の滝

■万博記念公園 自然文化園 ……………………… 46
万博の森／人間がつくった森／重なる木々たちの森／
地上十数センチに浮かぶ長ベンチ／
ススキのあいさつ／森と人間と水の大蛇／
滝がつたえたいこと／飛び石は、水面に浮いている／
赤褐色の時空を超えて／浅瀬の出会い／
錠前と鍵の風景／ふたつがみっつ／
森の空中回廊で、子どもたちは猿になる／
森の空中回廊で、子どもたちは鳥になる

設計資料・データ ……………………………………… 74

Contents

A love of intermediate nature ……………………………………… 3
Sweeping planes surrounded by woods ………………………… 4
Waterscapes nurturing life and interconnections ……………… 8
Miracle marsh connects us to life forces ………………………… 10
A vertical garden connecting the heavens and earth ………… 12
At the foot of the skyscrapers, new traditions await us ……… 14
Landscapes of relationships, alliances and fusion …………… 16

Shirotori Garden ……………………………………… 18
The shifting of the water's edge/Floating on water/
A cosmos hidden within the Garden of Tides

Garden of Reeds —
Osaka International Conference Center ……………… 24
Split the darkness/A cluster of enlightened reeds

A mid-wild forest — New Umeda City ……………… 30
Water of the city's birth/Held earth/
A dislocation of the building/Nine waterfalls/
Beyond the cascade/Banquet beneath the pavement/
Square, circle and triangle/Reverse waterfall

Natural and Cultural Gardens —
Expo '70 Commemorative Park ……………………… 46
Expo forest/Man-made forest/Layered wood/
Some 10cm off the ground/Greetings of the *susuki* grass/
Forest, man and water serpent/Message from the waterfall/
Stepping stones floating on water/
Spanning rust-colored time and space/
Encounter in shallow waters/
Lock-and-key landscape/Two to three/
Children become monkeys on the sky walk in the canopy/
Children become birds on the sky walk in the canopy

Design materials/Data ……………………………………… 74

中くらいの自然

わたしは、中くらいの自然が好きだ。
日本人が描く自然には、
大自然と小自然との間を行き来する尺度を転換するときの、
ときめきの美学があるように思う。
大海原の大自然には、
文句なしにその偉大さを感じひれ伏してしまう。
その大海原を日本庭園では、砂紋の小自然に縮めて表現する。
しかし、枯山水の庭には入り込めないもどかしさがある。
百寿の梅の盆栽は、時を縮めた大自然だが、
鶯はそこでは雛をかえすことができない。
私たちの日常の世界で、自然と親しむのは大自然でも、
小自然でもなく、その中間にある「中自然」にあると思う。
それほどの昔ではなくても、街にはトンボが飛び交い、
小川にはメダカが泳いでいた。
子どもたちは、そのなかに入りこんで、遊んでいた。
人間と自然が同じ背丈で交わっていた。
この中くらいの自然が、めっきり少なくなった。
中くらいの自然は、生きものたちの暮らしの場だ。
その生きものたちの暮らしの場と人間の暮らしの場とが、
日常の世界で共生できる。この「中自然」を、呼び起こしたいと願う。
わたしは、この中自然を「風景」として捉える
「風景造園家」として活動してきた。
中自然の風景であれば、その風景は突然おしゃべりになる。
わたしも、詩人になれる。
この対話のある風景こそ、都市化による自然破壊の風景に
自然を再建するよすがになるのではないか。
このような想いをこめて、
みなさまにこれまでの小品をお届けしたい。

A love of intermediate nature

In describing Nature, I feel Japanese people hold a certain aesthetic, like a pulsating movement of scale transitioning between what we might call Grand nature and Micro-nature. We feel completely overwhelmed by the glory when we face something like the vast magnificence of the ocean.

A Japanese garden represents that ocean, reduced to micro-nature through the use of sand. However, when we are given only this reduced version of nature, known as *karesansui*, we inevitably feel an impenetrable irritation inside of us. While we can consider an ancient bonsai plum tree to be the work of Grand nature, the bush warbler would not even be able to hatch her chicks in its branches.

In our every day lives, intimacy with nature has been neither Grand nor Micro-nature; if nothing else the dragonflies have been flying about, the *medaka* fish have been swimming in the small streams. And amidst this scene, our children have enjoyed themselves in play. An equal relationship has existed between humans and nature.

This kind of intermediate nature has declined considerably these days. The nature found within intermediate nature is where living creatures create their niches and survive. Wildlife habitats and our human habitat are able to coexist on an everyday basis. For this reason, I feel I must make my appeal now, an appeal on behalf of what I call "intermediate nature."

I have been working as a 'landscape architect' who regards intermediate nature as a 'landscape' in and of itself.
As a landscape, intermediate nature holds its own voice and can converse with us.

I am also a poet. Might we imagine that this very landscape, which we can interact with and bring into discussion, may be able to aid in the recovery process and revival of nature, in spite of that landscape which is destroying nature through urbanization?

With such a notion in mind, I would like to introduce you to some of my works so far.

森に囲まれた平坦で広い空地

失われた森と空地

　平地にある森は失われた。日本の森は、そのほとんどが山の厳しい斜面にしかない。かつては丘に、平野に森があった。武蔵野の雑木林はその典型だった。森は住まいの端に追いやられてしまった。人間が山を削り谷を埋めてつくった造成地には、建物がぎっしりと詰まっていて、もはや森の居場所はなくなってしまった。私たちの文化は、平地から平地の森に歩み入る感性をえることができなくなった。

森に囲まれた空っぽの空間

　森にとり囲まれた何もない広い平らな空地。日常の空間ではそのような空地は見あたらない。平らで何もない空間は、未利用地とみられる。人は、そこにいつか建物が建ち、耕作地として使われないと、もったいないと考える。平地の少ない日本では、空っぽの空間は「空き地」であり、役に立っていない土地、無駄な土地と見てしまう。

　しかし、森に囲まれた何もない広い空間ほど、人間に不可欠なものはない。

　そこでは人びとが開放され、太陽のもとで日常から開放されている姿がみられる。建物や人工物がないからこそ、平らな広場に価値がある。無用の用が、森に囲まれた空地だ。

森は故郷

　森はたんなる空地の背景ではない。人は森に背をむけて座り、視線を空地に投げかける。森はいつか帰るべき故郷なのだ。背をむけるのは、森が人を襲ってこないからだ。森がつくる空地は、人が人にかえる舞台。そこには、太陽と星空と月と、草むら

しなる石畳と湾曲する水辺、丸い灌木たちが森へと誘う／Gently waving stepping stones, the curved waterside and pruned shrubs invite us into the woods.

森の中へと丸い灌木たちが迎える
Pruned round shrubs lead to the woods.

樹林と丸い灌木たちが、水流を明るい広場へ導く
Trees and shrubs guide the stream into the open space.

大地の起伏に屹立する大樹／ Gigantic trees in the soft undulations of the open space.

大樹の木陰での休息／ Taking time out under a magnificent tree.

森を背にして、ヒトは休息／ Having a rest behind the woods.

Sweeping planes surrounded by woods

Lost forests and open spaces

Flat, wooded areas have vanished from the landscape. Most of Japan's forested lands exist on steep mountain slopes. There used to be woods on hills and flat areas. Musashino Coppice Wood was representative of this. Humans developed this land by leveling off the mountains and filling in valleys, while the area became dense with buildings — no longer a place suitable for woodlands to flourish. It became impossible for us to feel that traditional sense of entering into the woods, after it all became level ground.

Empty open-space surrounded by woods

If empty lands are not used for building or cultivation, they are felt to be merely wasted spaces. In Japan, where flat spaces are limited, the only empty, open spaces are considered 'vacant land,' which ultimately means useless or derelict.

However, there is nothing more indispensable to human beings than expansive empty space.

People feel a sense of freedom under the sunshine there. The very fact there are no buildings or man-made objects gives value to these flat open spaces. Indeed, the proverb about "seeing the useful in that which seems useless" applies to any of these open spaces surrounded by woods.

Our roots in the woods

The woods are not merely backdrops for the open spaces. People sit with their backs to the woods, gazing upon the open spaces that expand in front of them. We expect to ultimately return to the woods at some point. We can sit with our backs facing the woods because we know they would never turn on us. That open space, created by the woods, is the stage upon which people meet their truly human element. The sun, the stars, the moon and the grass all meet there, to interact with one another. The relationships between new lives are developed here.

Open spaces link us to the gods

In Japan, there has been a tradition of these wide open spaces

引き裂かれた大地のなかの飛び石のある水流が、森へと導く
A stream with stepping stones between split ground guides visitors into the woods.

との出会いがある。新しいいのちのつながりと出会いがある。

神とつながる空地

　日本にはもともと森に囲まれた何もない空地の文化があった。森に囲まれた奈良の春日大社に、もともと社殿建築はなかった。あったのは森に囲まれたただの空地だった。そこに神が降臨し、人はそこで神と出会った。その神が降臨する森の空地につながる神への道があった。参道である。京都の下鴨神社は、二川が合流する氾濫の河原に育った落葉樹の森に囲まれている。この明るい森を参道が空を直線に切りとって、神域を突き刺すように伸びている。直線の空と参道が交差したところに神がおわします。

森を出てヒトになった

　ヒトは森を出て人になった。ヒトの祖先である霊長類は森の樹上生活者だった。地上に降り立った霊長類は、森から草原に出るときに二足歩行形態に身体を改造し、手が解放されて知的動物・人になった。森に囲まれた草原は、ヒトが人になった起源の地なのだ。現代、森に囲まれた広々とした空地は、ゴルフ場の風景だ。ゴルフのゲームは、森を出たヒトが草原で草食動物を射止める生存の闘いを遊びへと転換したものだ。森に囲まれた広大で平らな風景こそ、私たち人類の起源の地なのだ。この原風景を、万博記念公園でつくった。

そして、森へ帰ろう

　空地を背にして森に帰ろう。森の入口には丸い刈り込みの潅木群がやさしく迎えてくれる。森へといざなう水の道。巨樹のもとにいこう。
　広い空地にひかれた水と飛び石の道。その水・道が空地と森とをつないでくれる。

水源を求めて、森に帰ろう
Let us return to the woods to find the springs.

surrounded by woods. Originally, there was no shrine constructed upon the expansive area of Kasuga Taisha in Nara, also surrounded by woods. What existed there was only this empty open space and the surrounding woods. This is where the gods made their descent and the people could interact with them. The approach to this open space through the forest is known as the *sandou*. Shimogamo Shrine in Kyoto is surrounded by a wooded area of deciduous trees growing in the flood plain between two rivers. The *sandou* cuts straight through these striking woods, leading into the sacred precinct. The gods exist right at the point where the sky line meets the *sandou*.

Emerging from the woods and evolving into modern man
The Hominidae emerged from the forests and became human. Their ancestors the primates, spent their lives in the tree branches, but once primates stepped down onto the ground and ventured out of the woods and into the grasslands, they began their evolution into upright, bi-pedal creatures with two free arms. They eventually became highly intelligent animals known as human beings. The grasslands surrounded by wooded grounds are the very place where Homo sapiens evolved into human beings. Today, the large open spaces surrounded by woods have become golf courses. The game of golf changed the battle of survival on the grassy fields into play, and humans who once emerged from the woods now win over the herbivores. It is from these large wide-open tracts of land bordered by wooded areas that we humans actually originate. This is the sort of landscape I have designed for the Osaka International Exposition Memorial Park.

Now, let us return to the woods
Let us now turn away from the open spaces, and head back into the woods. The entrance to the woods warmly welcomes us with clusters of rounded, pruned shrubs. The waterways tempt us into the woods. Let's go to where the giant trees are. Waterways and stepping stones that lure us into the open will lead the way, water creates the connection between the open land and the woods.

四角い飛び石のある水流が、森を引き裂く／A stream with square shaped stepping stones splits the woods.

小川が森を育み、子どもたちに命を伝える／The stream nurtures the woods and shows life to children.

いのちを育み、つなぐ水辺と水面

水面と水辺は風景の魔術師

　水辺は、森と野と水面とをつなぐ場所。水面は空を映し、巨樹を映し、太陽の輝きを映す。雲を映す。映すことで、それぞれはつながりを増幅させる。水面と水辺は風景の魔術師だ。水辺に立つと、そこには群集はいない。

帝国主義の庭

　ルイ14世がつくらせたフランスのヴェルサイユ宮殿の広大な庭は、すべてが直線と円で形づくられ、その中心に太陽王が世界に光を放つ帝国主義の権力の美の庭園であった。見栄と虚飾なしには、群集で満ち溢れたこの庭には入れない。

隠遁の楽園・明日への湧園

　マリー・アントワネットは、ヴェルサイユ宮殿を逃れて隠遁の水辺のある小さな田舎をつくって、孤独な楽園を楽しんだ。
　水辺は人を文明の抑圧と桎梏から解き放つ。文明の圧力が高まれば、人は大きな広がりのある、誰もが入り込めない静寂の世界に自己を解きほぐそうとする。そこは隠者の楽園ではなく、明日を生きる力の湧園なのだ。

いのちを育み、つなぐ水辺

　いのちを育み、空と大地と池をつなぐ水辺は、自然の不規則性から生まれる。不規則性は、中心がないこと、中心を避けて秩序を生み出すこと。それは反逆の文明化だ。

夕日を映す反逆の水面

　反逆の庭は、後水尾天皇の修学院離宮庭園に見ることができる。都市に閉じ込められた小さな山水の庭を飛び出し、遠い山々、沈む夕日を借景として取り入れた開かれた庭。山腹に広大な池をつくり、そこに舟を浮かべた。闇夜の水面を照らす月明りは、権力への反逆ののろしだった。

万博記念公園の水面の庭は、自然と共存する未来の文明を予感させる

　万博記念公園の多彩な水辺と水面がつなぐ、いのちのつながりの風景。それは、人間の手で惹き起している地球温暖化が地球の生態系を破壊し、ついには人間をも滅ぼしてしまう破壊的な行き過ぎの文明を押しとどめようとする反逆の意志が込められている。なぜなら、6,400万人を集めた日本万国博覧会のパビリオン群を消し去った跡に建設された万博記念公園の水辺の庭は、自然とそして地球と共存できる未来を託されて登場したからだ。
　「庭とは、長い長い年月を通じて人類の文明が至福の概念を自然のうちに刻み込まれた手段である」という言葉がある。この水面の庭が、持続可能な文明の未来を照らす鏡になってほしい。

孤高の大樹が水面に映しだされる／A single, lonely tree is reflected on the water's surface.

大空と水面をつなぐ大樹たち
Towering trees connect the sky and the water surface.

Waterscapes nurturing life and interconnections

The water's edges and surfaces are landscape magicians
The waterside is where the woods, the meadows and the surface of the water all come together. The surface of the water reflects the sky, the giant trees, the sunshine, and the clouds. Through these reflections, each one of these connections is amplified. The waters' edges and surfaces are the magicians of landscape. Standing on the waterside, there are no crowds to be found.

An imperialistic garden
The vast garden built by Louis XIV at the Versailles Palace in France, entirely designed using straight lines and circles, is a magnificent garden of imperialistic power where the rays of the Sun King emanate from the center throughout the world. One cannot enter this garden, teeming with crowds, without his pomp and ostentatiousness.

Secluded paradise, comforting oasis for tomorrow
Marie Antoinette escaped the Palace at Versailles and built a small rustic villa where she could find solitude by the water's edge. She enjoyed her reclusive paradise there. Spending time near water releases people from the oppressions and fetters of civilization. When the pressures of everyday life build up, we try to unwind in a calm environment of open air where no one else can enter. It is not a paradise of escape but a comforting oasis that gives us the strength to carry on… into tomorrow.

Encouraging life, the waterside connects
With its natural irregularities, the waterside fosters life while creating a connection between the sky, the earth and water. Irregularity, in the sense that there is no center, and in fact an order emerges out of the avoidance of any center — the civilized rebellion.

A subversive water surface reflects the setting sun
An example of this kind of typical garden can be seen at Shugaku-in Imperial Villa, constructed by the retired Emperor Go-mizunoo. Surrounded by the city, a small *sansui* garden appears, borrowing the scenery of the distant hills and sunset to complete its design. A large pond was built on the hillside where boats were sailed. The moonlight illuminating the surface of the water on a dark evening is the surest sign of how this garden resists authority.

Water gardens at Osaka Expo '70 Commemorative Park predict harmony with nature for our future
The connections made between the diverse waterscapes at Osaka Expo '70 Commemorative Park is a background for the relationships formed between life forces. This is an expression of resistance, an effort to stand up against the destructive extremes of a civilization responsible for causing climate change by its own hand while destroying the earth's natural ecosystems and eventually leading to the extinction of mankind. This is because the water garden at Osaka Expo '70 Commemorative Park, built from the ruins of the Japan World Exposition pavilions where a crowd of 64 million people once gathered, is the entryway to a future that is committed to harmony between the natural world and man.

It is said that, "gardens are a means by which, over many long years, humans have been able to carve out a supreme bliss through connecting with nature." It is my hope that these waterscapes become mirrors reflecting the future of sustainable civilization.

水面に浮かぶ飛び石たち
Stepping stones emerge from out of the water.

浮かぶ飛び石たちの間を小魚が群れる
Little fish inhabit the spaces between the stepping stones.

地上の生きものたちを映す水面
The water surface reflects the life that grows in the earth.

奇跡の沼が、いのちをつなぐ

山水の風景が失われた

　山水を枯山水という砂と岩の無機物で固めることで、日本庭園は大自然を身近に楽しむ精神を育んだ。

　工業化は、日本の都市から田舎までの河川や小川を、三面張りの無機物のコンクリート製に変えた。しかし、この人工物に自然を感じることはない。

鎮守の森

　日本人の山水には中くらいの自然がない。あるとすれば、鎮守の森だ。人間と神がつくった悠久の聖なる森だ。しかし、この森は、入らずの森だ。立ち入ることができない。陽の差し込まない暗い森に、鳥や昆虫などの生きものは少ない。

遠い記憶の沼を再現

　誰でもが入り込め、自由に散策ができ、陽光が差し込み、明るく、ゆったりと散歩ができる深い森がほしい。ホタルが乱舞し、小鳥が歌い、小魚が泳ぐ森の中の静寂の森である。そこでひらめいたのが、私たちがとうの昔に記憶の彼方に押し込めた「沼」だった。

アメリカ館の跡地に奇跡の沼

　ビオトープという自然回復の言葉が1990年代にドイツから輸入される20年も前の1971年、万博記念公園に「渡りの沼」という名の生態系再建の自然地を設計した。万博当時、月の石を展示して最大の人気を集めたアメリカ館の跡地であった。

　1970年代に、そこに沼ができたのは、奇跡だった。当時の国の方針では、公園に沼をつくることは許されなかった。私はこの沼を「奇跡の沼」と呼びたい。

未来を暗示する沼

　この沼こそ、日本の進むべき道を示している。レイチェル・カーソン女史が化学物質によって鳥さえも鳴かなくなった環境汚染を告発した『沈黙の春』は、ミナマタの悲劇と同じ60年代。70年代の世界の工業国は、公害に苦しめられていた。大量生産・大量消費、大量廃棄の時代の落とし子である公害の反省のもと、万博跡地は自然の文化園になった。

土の道に寄り添う小川
A stream runs beside the footpath.

木漏れ日の中の小川
A stream catches the sunlight streaming in through the leaves.

森の中の小川
A stream runs through the woods.

Miracle marsh connects us to life forces

Loss of hill and water landscapes
The Japanese garden has cultivated the spirit of closely communing with Grand Nature through the *karesansui* style garden, which expresses hills and water through the arrangement of inanimate objects, namely sand and stone.

Sacred village groves
For Japanese people, there is no intermediate nature in the hills and waters. It is rather found in the groves at village shrines. It is found in the eternal sacred forests that have been created by both humans and the gods. However, entry into the forests is forbidden. No one can go inside. And, because the sun does not reach into these dark wooded areas, there are few birds and insects living in them.

Recreating a marsh out of fading memories
I want to design deep woods, where all feel welcome to enter, and happily stroll about taking in the light of the sun. They would echo the marshes we hold deep in our memories from long ago, still and peaceful woods where fireflies dance about noisily, small birds sing and little fish inhabit the streams.

Miracle marsh replaces the abandoned US pavilion
In 1971, more than 20 years before the word 'biotope' was imported from Germany in the 1990s, I created the Migratory Marsh at Osaka Expo '70 Commemorative Park, a natural zone modeled to replicate an ecosystem. It was developed on the vacant lot of the Expo's American pavilion, which had been hugely popular for exhibiting a moonstone. Realization of this marsh on that site in the 1970s was a miracle. Constructing a marsh on parklands was not allowed in the national policies at that time. I want to call this the "Miracle Marsh".

A marsh that foretells the future
The marsh demonstrates exactly the way in which Japan should advance. *Silent Spring* is the book in which Rachel Carson alleged that chemicals were the cause of environmental contamination that stopped even the birds from singing. This came out around the same time as the Minamata tragedy in the 1960s. Reflecting upon the aftermath of an era of mass production, mass consumption, and mass waste, this vacant land that was once the site of Expo '70 was turned into a natural and cultural park.

アメリカ館の跡地の「渡りの沼」
Migratory Marsh at the abandoned US pavilion.

沼を横切る
View out over the marsh.

水面に映し出されたメタセコイアの巨樹／Colossal metasequoia trees are reflected in the water.

天と地をつなぐ垂直の庭園

超高層建築の谷間で

　大都会の中心は、超高層建築群で覆われている。人びとは数百メートルのビルの暗く、冷たい谷間に押しひしがれて急ぎ足に歩む。だから人びとは温かく明るい地下に逃げ込む。人間が超高層建築に押しつぶされ、自然が押しつぶされ、太陽と星空が地上から奪われた。

　大都会の庭は、もはや失われようとしていた。日本庭園は背景にある山水を借景にしてのびやかに造られた。しかし、大都会には山水の借景はない。超高層ビルの屋上にのぼってはじめて、遠望の彼方に山水が望まれる。

文明を借景にして山水を呼びもどせ！

　大都会には、かつてあった山水の記憶すらない。私たちは生まれながら、人工の文明しか見たことがなく育ってきた。

　失われた山水を、超高層建築群にこそ取り戻したい。それには、超高層建築が、大都会に失われた山水をよびもどす借景になるべきだ。

　昔の人が山水を借景にして文明を築いたように、現代のわたしたちは、文明を借景にして山水を描くのだ。

天と地をつなぐ垂直の庭園

　現代の庭は、超高層建築の形に、大自然のいのちの循環を刻み込むことで、大都会を蘇らせる力に変えることができる。これが、「新梅田シティ」の天と地をつなぐ垂直の庭園のドラマだ。

　巨大な工業製品、工業デザインの超高層建築。その頂上階にも届かんとするステンレスの９本の円柱のてっぺんから噴き出す落水が、地上の乾いた九つの岩を穿つ。落水と岩は歓喜と祈りの叫びをあげて、大地に滋養を届ける。

舞台をつくる布滝

　新梅田シティの花畑、樹木、噴水、流れ、稲田を潤した水は、聖なる布滝となって、水と岩とのつながりを祝福する。天と地を結ぶドラマの背景だ。

　布滝の裏は、超高層建築の足許の隠れ家だ。人は開閉自在の水のカーテンから時折見せる森と水辺を一人占めして、ひとときのやすらぎを満喫する。

空中庭園を背にして噴き出す水が、中自然の森の木々を潤す／Cascading into the sky garden background, a waterfall offers sustenance to the mid-wild forest.

左／勢いよく水を噴き出す列柱たち／Waterfalls cascade from stainless steel pillars.　右／９本の列柱滝は、地上の岩を穿ち、いのちの水になる／Waterfalls cascade out of nine stainless steel pillars, piercing the dry rocks at the base and becoming a vital water source.

A vertical garden connecting the heavens and earth

In the valley of the skyscrapers
Skyscraper architecture has become the central point of any large city. People are weighed down by the gloom of these towering structures and hurriedly run around in the cold valleys they create. To escape this darkness, people escape to the warmth and bright lighting of the underground shopping malls. Humans and nature are overstressed; we can no longer see the sun and the starlit sky from the ground.

The gardens and natural areas in the great cities were already vanishing. The Japanese garden was magnificently designed to borrow the scenic backdrop of the distant hills and water. On the other hand, this means that there is no natural scenery left in the great cities.

Borrowing scenes from civilization, we must recreate the hills and water
In a huge city, we can no longer recall the hills and water that were once there. From the day we are born, we exist in a culture surrounded by man-made, artificial objects. I wish to respond to this skyscraper culture by working to bring back the hills and waterscapes to our big cities. The skyscrapers should now phase out and become the scenic backdrop while the hills and waters are renewed.

People long ago built their civilizations with the hills and waterways as the background scenery but we in the modern world will create hills and waterscapes that put all that into our background.

A vertical garden connecting the heavens and earth
Based on skyscraper forms, modern gardens can revive big cities with their power by sculpting a model of how life circulates within Grand nature. This is the drama of the vertical garden in New Umeda City, which aims to create a link between the sky and the earth. This skyscraper architecture is the result of mass industrial products and industrial design. A waterfall cascades from the top of nine stainless steel pillars that represent skyscrapers piercing into nine dry rocks at the base. The waterfalls and rocks cry out in joy and hope, offering nourishment to the land below them.

A waterfall sets the stage
The water flowing through fields of flowers, trees and shrubs, fountains, canals, waterways and rice fields at New Umeda City becomes sacred, finally cascading down to celebrate the relationships between the waterscapes and rocks. It is a scene depicting the drama that bonds the heavens with the earth. Behind the waterfall and at the foot of the skyscrapers, there lies a hiding place. People freely enter a wooded scene created behind a curtain of water, a place where they can fully take in a moment of peace and tranquility.

左／幅40mの布滝は、中自然の舞台をつくる緞帳
A waterfall of 40 meters width is the drop curtain that sets the mid-wild stage.
右／布滝の緞帳が開く。その裏で食事を楽しむ
The waterfall curtain rises. A man enjoys his meal behind it.

超高層建築の下の新しい伝説

超高層建築は、宇宙に飛びたつロケット

　超高層建築は、土地の記憶を消しさってもよいのか。宇宙に向けて発射するロケットのように、地球の富のすべてを収奪したエネルギーによって屹立する超高層建築。超高層建築は進歩を謳歌するモニュメント。しかし、超高層建築は、地球の自然資本を食い尽くす怪物的巨人。

高層建築の地べたの野仏

　わたしたちは、この巨人に、大地の豊かさと伝説の滋養からすくすく育つ竹のように、大空に伸びていく姿を見たい。超高層建築が立ち上がる地べたは、いのちを潤す野の風景でありたい。野こそ、小川が流れ、小動物たちの息遣いを嗅ぎわけることができる。人びとは、野に踏み出し、野に生きざまを晒し、野に死に、そして自然に戻るのだ。そして野はまた新たな生命を生みだす。超高層建築の大地への噴射が、宇宙と地べたのいのちがつながっていることの証しとして、鎮魂の祈りをささげよう。それが、野の野仏たちだ。

石畳の下の干潟

　超高層建築の地べたの石畳をめくると、埋立地の前の干潟の風景が顔をのぞかせた。三葉虫も一緒だ。5億年前の海の生き物たちの上にわたしたちの生がある。超高層建築に働き、そこに集う人びとは、地べたを散策するとき、いま見たこの干潟の隙間から海底を覗くがよい。そこでは海につながる進化の風景を辿れるのだ。

石器時代人の記憶

　わたしたちの文明は、石器時代人の知能と技を受け継いでいる。彼らの岩窟の住まいを避けて、超高層建築は建設された。大地に刻印された「いにしえの足跡」が、超高層建築にいのちを注ぎ込んでいる。

空中庭園を中自然の森から見上げる
Looking up at the sky garden from the mid-wild forest.

空中庭園の足許にうずくまる野仏（F・ボナルディ 作）
A sculpture at the foot of the sky garden.

At the foot of the skyscrapers, new traditions await us

Rockets taking off into space

I wonder if it is acceptable? The skyscrapers have totally removed our recollections of the land. Like rockets catapulting into space, skyscrapers tower above us all using an energy that plunders the earth of all her precious treasures. While they are monuments celebrating human advancement, they are at the same time monstrous beings devouring the earth's natural resources.

Skyscraper sculptures rooted in bare earth

We like to watch these giants rise up into the heavens, like fast-growing bamboo taking their nourishment from the fertile fields and the power of legends. All the while, we hope the ground from which these skyscrapers emerge is still teeming with biological diversity. We hope those fields remain buzzing with flowing streams and tiny living creatures. We take our first steps on the soil, build our lives upon the soil, die and eventually return back to the soil. The soil, the earth then bears new life all over again. Let us remember those who have passed on from this life with these structures that climb upward toward the sky as the symbol that a deep bond exists between the heavens and the earth. These sculptures also have their origins in the earth.

石畳の下に干潟が顔をのぞかせる／The tide pools emerge from under the pavement.

Paving over the tide pools

When the pavement at the base of a skyscraper is stripped off, you will notice there had once been a tidal flat, which was lost due to landfill. Trilobites have also found this spot. We share our existence with creatures that lived in the seas some 500 million years ago. While strolling about, people living and working in the skyscrapers should take a peek beneath the sea, to glimpse what can be understood in the crevices of these tidal flats. This is where we find how our evolution is connected to the seas.

Recalling stone age man

Our modern day society is a continuation of the intelligence and artistry of Stone Age man. They left their cave residences…and the skyscrapers were built. It is from the ancient footprints they left imprinted into the land that our skyscrapers have been infused with life.

右／顔をむきだす野仏 (F・ボナルディ 作)
A sculpture
左／瞑想する野仏 (F・ボナルディ 作)
A sculpture seemingly lost in meditation.

中自然の森の崖に彫られた舞う人びとの彫像 (富永敦也 作)／A statue of dancing people carved into a cliff in the mid-wild forest.

野仏のおなかの中に別の顔が (F・ボナルディ 作)
A face for its stomach.

つながり、むすびあい、溶け込む風景

真昼の一服
建物を突き抜けて
竹林が整列している
建物の後ろには
茶畑がうねっている
茶畑のうねりの波が
建物のなかで
竹林の直線を創りだしている
しかし、その直線は
竹林のトンネル
トンネルをくぐると
その先にあるのが、お茶の世界
いざなわれた紅のなかで
真昼の一服

おすましさんの竹
竹は垂直に
上に向かって伸びあがる
風にそよいで、すましている
シルバーの皮膜は巨大ドーム
こちらは、ランの花の展示会場を覆っている
深い紅のランを包む
柔らかいシルバーのドームに
おすましさんの竹が
寄り添う
その足下に

ラベンダーが広がる
ラベンダー、ドーム、竹
三つの異なる色彩が
青い空のもとで、溶けあう

お互いの三角
山際から染みだす
三角の出っ張り
シルバーのドームから
染みだすラベンダーの三角
染みだす三角が
土に三角を生みだす
互いの三角が
互いの三角と
しっかり結びつけられる

三角たちの握手
三角たちの抱擁
大地に刻まれた
愛のしるし

茶畑を背景にした建物の中を突き抜ける竹の参道
An approach of bamboo passes by a house with tea plantations in the background.

竹林の参道
Bamboo-lined approachway.

Landscapes of relationships, alliances and fusion

A break at midday
Piercing through the building
A grove of neatly lined bamboo
Behind the house —
Rolling tea plantations
The rolling waves create
A grove of bamboo in perfectly straight rows
In the building
A tunnel of bamboo
And passing through this tunnel,
At the very end —
A world of tea
In the enticing crimson red
A break at midday

Oh, virtuous bamboo
Upright, the bamboo
Climbs upward into the heavens
Swaying in the wind, modestly
Its silver canopy creates a giant dome,
Concealing an orchid display
Wrapped in the deep red colour of the orchids —
And in this gentle silver dome,
The unassuming bamboo
Nestle together
At their base
Lavender sprouts out
Lavender, the dome, the bamboo —
Against a sky of blue sky, this fusion of color

Mutual triangles
Exude forth from the mountain range
Protruding triangles
Pour forth from that dome of silver
A triangle of lavender
A triangle manifests
Giving birth to another triangle
Mutual triangles
Closely bonded, these triangles
Shake hands —
Embrace —
Etched upon the earth
A mark of love

シルバーに輝くドームを背にした
柔らかい竹林が撫ぜる
Soft bamboos mesh with the shining, silvery dome.

湧きあがるシルバーのドーム、空にのびあがる竹林、地を這う
ラベンダーの三角たちの競演
Competition between the silvery dome, the towering bamboos and the triangular lavender beds.

ラベンダーの三角たちと土の三角たちの結合
Triangles of lavender interact with triangle ground patterns.

白鳥庭園

Shirotori Garden

せめぎあう水辺

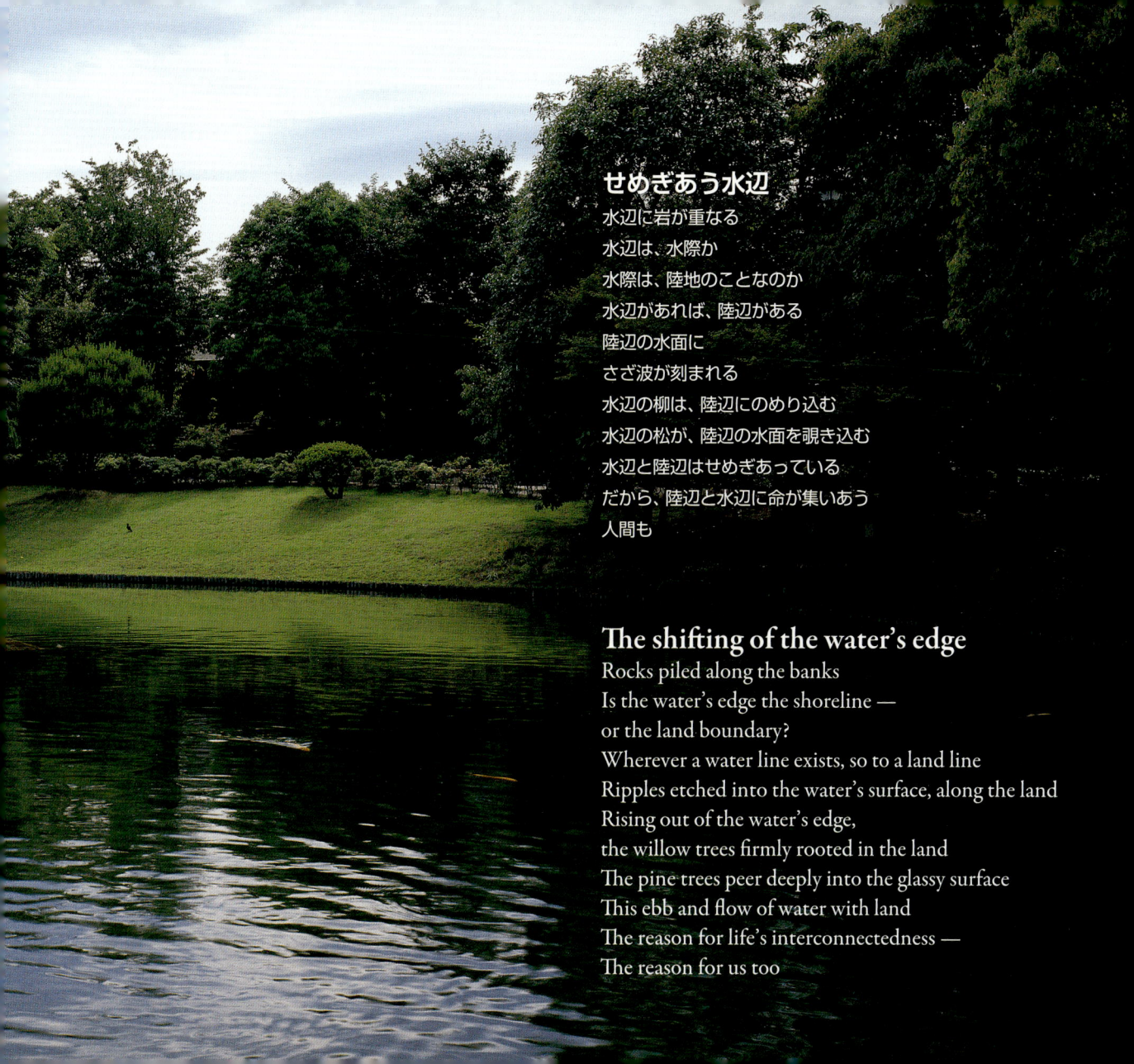

水辺に岩が重なる
水辺は、水際か
水際は、陸地のことなのか
水辺があれば、陸辺がある
陸辺の水面に
さざ波が刻まれる
水辺の柳は、陸辺にのめり込む
水辺の松が、陸辺の水面を覗き込む
水辺と陸辺はせめぎあっている
だから、陸辺と水辺に命が集いあう
人間も

The shifting of the water's edge

Rocks piled along the banks
Is the water's edge the shoreline —
or the land boundary?
Wherever a water line exists, so to a land line
Ripples etched into the water's surface, along the land
Rising out of the water's edge,
the willow trees firmly rooted in the land
The pine trees peer deeply into the glassy surface
This ebb and flow of water with land
The reason for life's interconnectedness —
The reason for us too

水面に浮かぶ

飛び石が、お茶の世界へいざなう
飛び石を伝って、お茶の世界にむかう
お茶の世界も、水面に浮かぶ
お茶の世界は、水面の世界
一期一会は、水面に包まれる
水面の起源を、森に見つけよう
森は水を蓄える
森からながれでる小川
そこに、伝い石が添えられている
ゆるいながれに、何をながそうか

Floating on water

Stepping stones usher us into the world of tea
It is these stones that bring you into the tea space —
A realm floating upon the water's surface
The tea world, reflected on a watery plane
The master's "one time, one meeting" is enveloped in the water surface
Let us search the woods for the origins of this glimmering water
For it is in the forest where the water is stored
A stream flows forth, out of the woods —
It's running waters trickle over rocks and pebbles
And what shall I add to this gentle flow?

汐入の庭に込められた宇宙

月の力が、地球に伝わる

潮の満ち干

地球の鼓動が、月に応える

潮の満ち干

それは、宇宙の営み

日常の中に

宇宙の営みを感じたい

なぜなら

人間も

宇宙の星屑から生まれたのだから

宇宙に起源をもつ人間が

宇宙に遊ぶ

汐入の庭には

生命の誕生物語が隠されている

A cosmos hidden within the Garden of Tides
The powers of the moon sway the earth
As the tides give and take —

    We experience the workings of the cosmos
    Because
    We too
    Are born of that cosmic stardust
    We too have our origins in that strange deep void
    We play there, in Shioiri Garden
    And we find hidden there, life's birth story

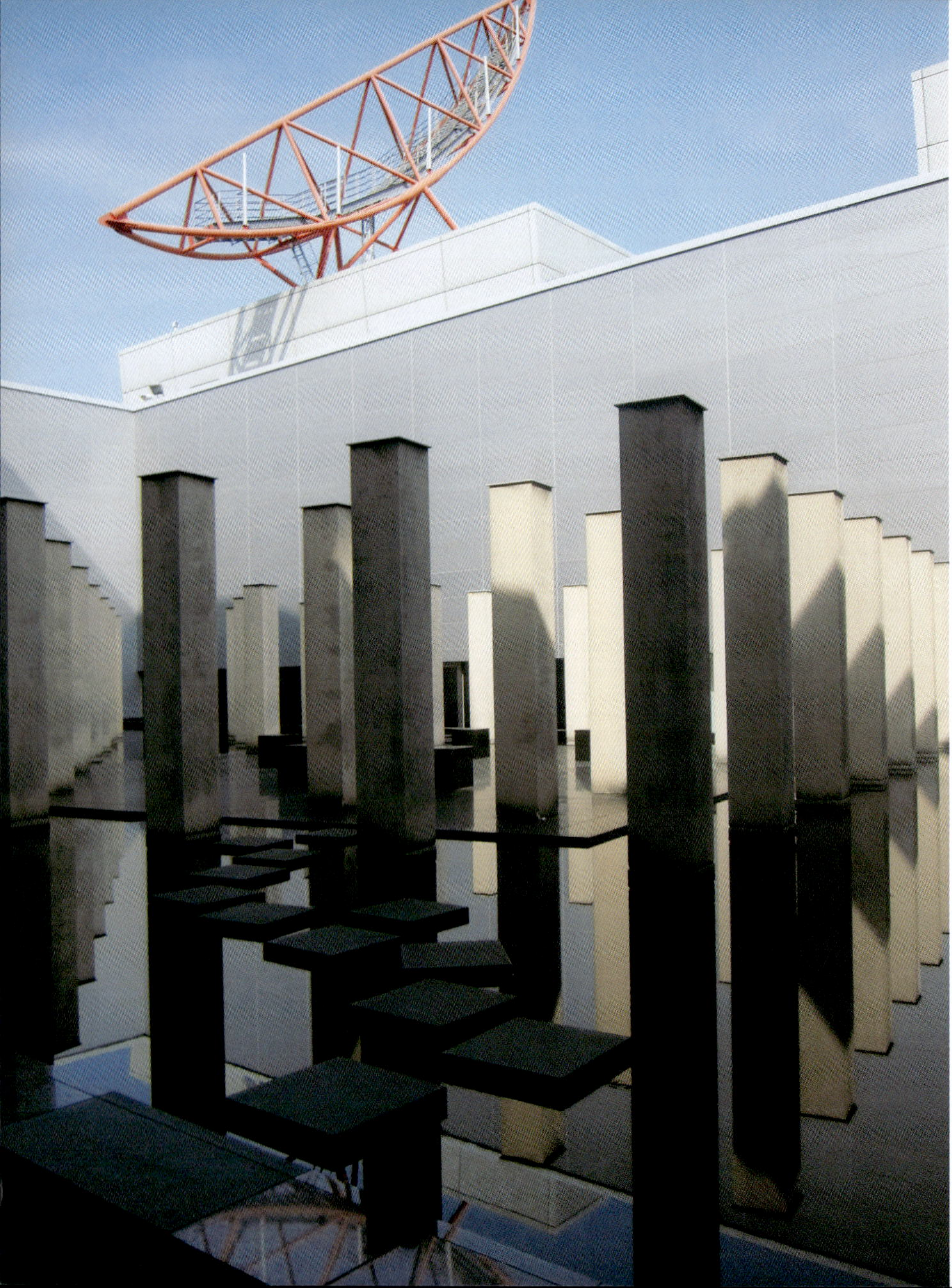
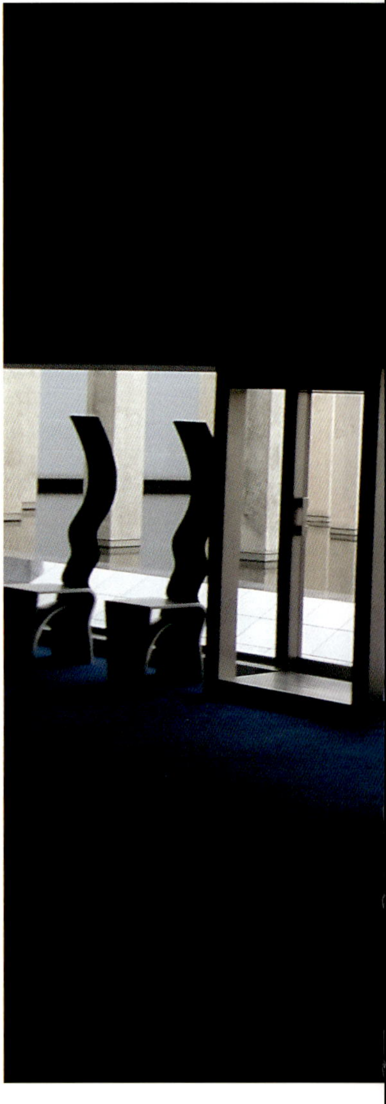

大阪府立国際会議場
葦原の庭

Garden of Reeds — Osaka International Conference Center

暗闇を引き裂く

暗黒を引き裂くジッパー
斜めの亀裂
亀裂の向こうに会議が踊る
賑わいのある柱
柱が踊る、柱がすべる
柱は
なにをしゃべっているのだろうか
柱は
水の中から生えている
柱は
陸に突き刺さっている
天空と水と大地を
串裂きにする柱ども
暗闇のさきに
なにがあるというのだ

Split the darkness

Zipper splits the darkness
A diagonal incision
Behind the crack, the Congress dances
in between dense pillars,
The pillars are dancing; they glide
What could they be talking about?
The pillars —
Towering up out of the water
The pillars —
Now piercing the land
The sky, the water and the land
Penetrated by the pillars
And what exists
beyond the darkness?

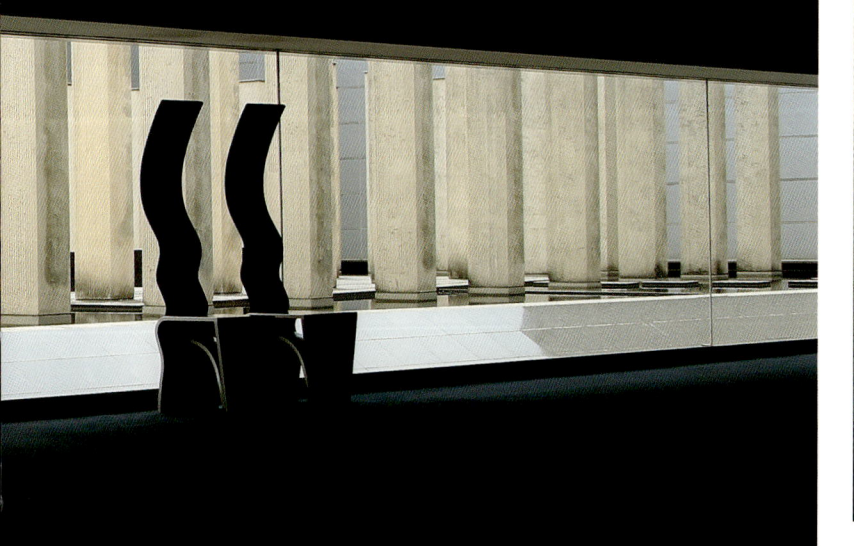

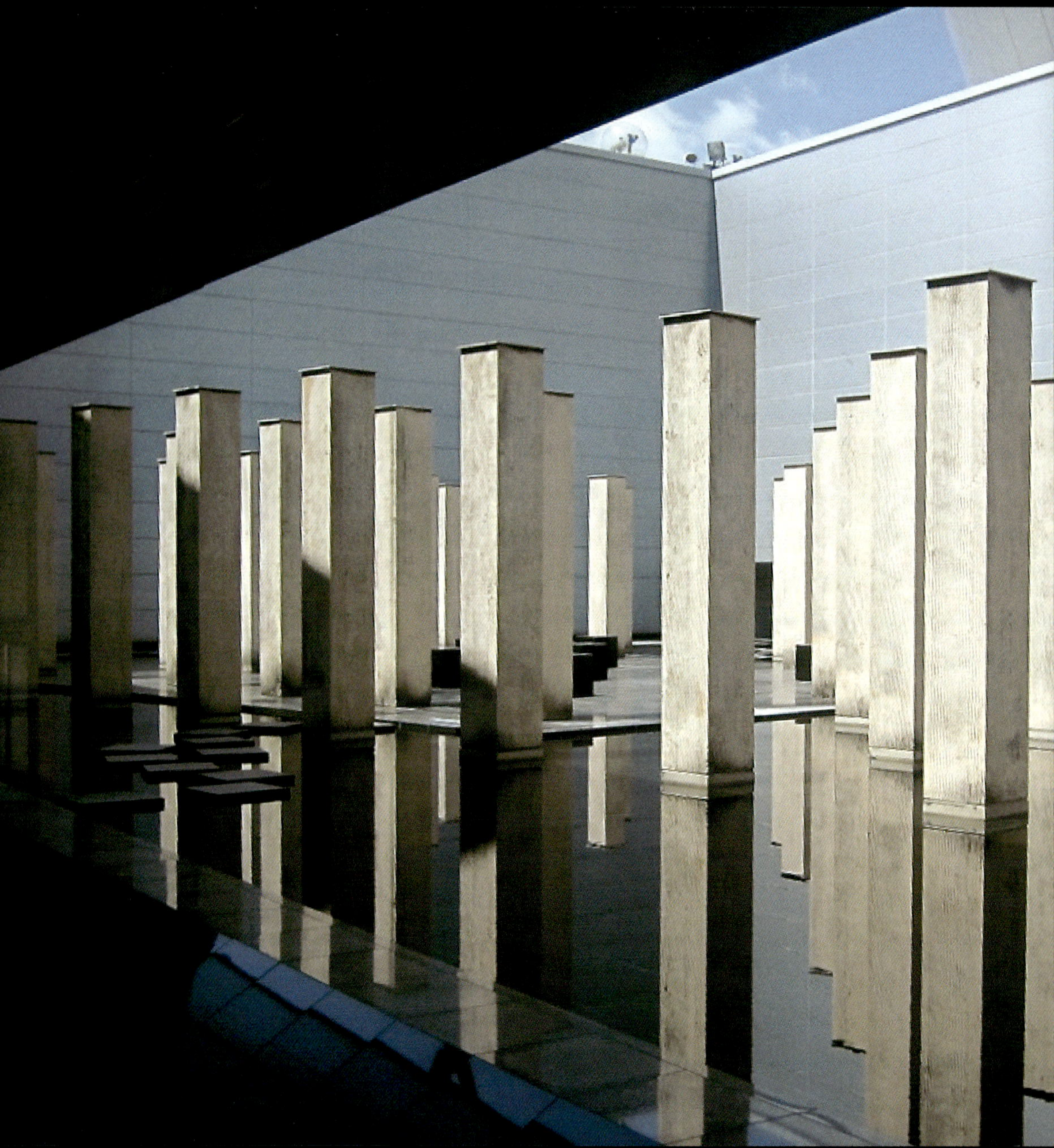

合理の葦の森

ごりごりごり
合理の葦の森が向こうに見える
合理の葦の森に行き着くまでに
揺らぎの石畳が水面に浮かぶ
思い切って飛び乗ってみる
ぎしぎしぎし
合理にはいると肌がこすれる
えい！
入ってしまえ！
合理のなかに、安寧を見つけたぞ
ひとときの安らぎのなかで、
希望を語ろう

A cluster of enlightened reeds

gori – gori – gori
A cluster of enlightened reeds
are seen in the distance
To reach these judicious reeds
Trembling stepping stones
that float on water
Be bold. Jump onto them —
gishi – gishi – gishi
So what if you scrape your skin —
entering into their wisdom
Enter wisely!
Within the soberness, we find peace
Let's sit back now —
And talk about our hopes

新梅田シティ
中自然の森

A mid-wild Forest — New Umeda City

都市の始まりの水

都市の始まりは
空中パラダイスから噴き出す
水ものがたり
都市の頂きに蓄えられた雨水が
空中の楽園を潤す
メタリックな噴出口から
地のいのちにむけて、
頂きの水が飛び出す

湾曲した九本の水しぶきが
地上の木々に降り注ぐ
風がまき上がり、梢をゆらし、
森は吠える
天とメタリックな楽園と地が
雨水でつながり、
都市に力を蘇らせる

**Water
of the city's birth**

Creation of a city
Gushing waters from
a sky paradise,
The water story —
Rainwater collected,
by the city
Offers a gift of moisture,
to the sky paradise
Out of the cascading
metallic spout
The water
Pours from the top
As the life force percolates
into the ground

Pouring down on the forest,
deeply rooted in earth
As winds ensue,
the treetops sway
The forest howls —
The heavens, the metallic
paradise and the earth
Bonded by rain showers,
To revive the city

抱かれた地球

超高層の都市の足下に
わたしたちの地球がある
都市が、地球を抱え込んでいる
渓谷、海洋、森林
草花、生きものたち
逆流滝、森の散策道、
木漏れ日
超高層都市の、ど真ん中に
出現した、わたしたちの地球だ
この地球に
超高層都市が蓄えた水を注ぐ
地球を劣化させない
その決意の証し

Held earth

Below the skyscrapers
Our Earth
The city holds the earth —
valleys, oceans, forests, fields of wildflowers,
all that is alive,
The reverse waterfall, wooded footpaths
sunbeams on leaves
In the very center of that skyscraper city
Our Earth appears
And, into this soil
Flows the water stored in the city
Proof of our determination
to prevent the Earth's decline

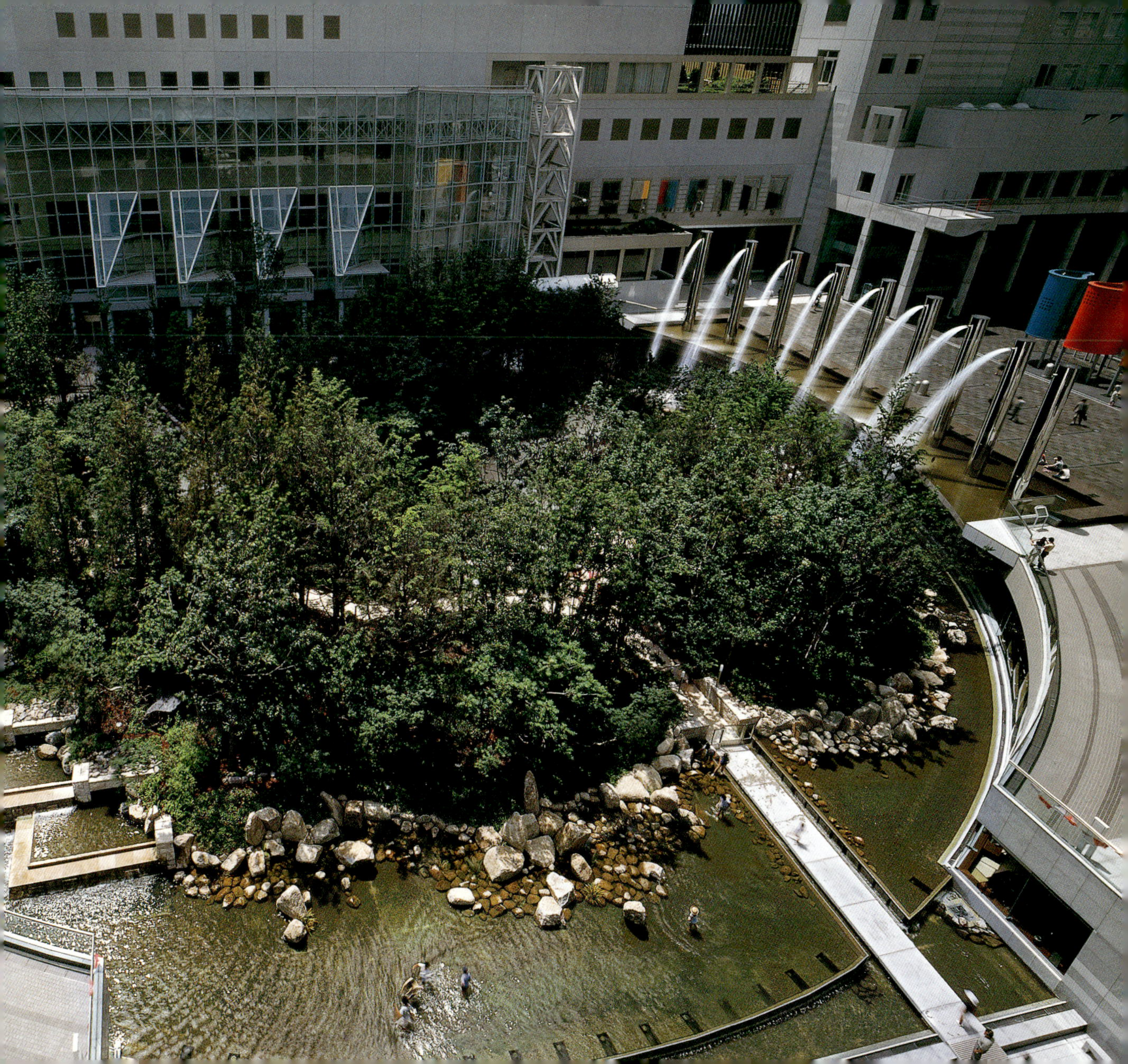

ビルの断層

ビルの断層に瀑布があらわれた
さあ！　水の舞台がととのうぞ
太陽にかがやく幕しずく
その前に役者が待っている
幕開けのほんのひととき
九つの役者たちは、それぞれ
地上のメタルの列柱に
何かを語りかける
さあ！　街の物語がはじまるぞ
準備はいいか
きらめく水の緞帳の前
のひととき

A dislocation of the building

At a dislocation of the building,
appears a waterfall
Now, the water theatre is ready
A curtain of water reflects the sunshine,
Actors wait in front of it,
Just a short time before the opening
Nine actors, respectively
Talking about something
To the nine metallic pillars
at ground level
Hey! The saga of the city begins
Are you ready?
Just a short moment
In front of a glistening curtain of water

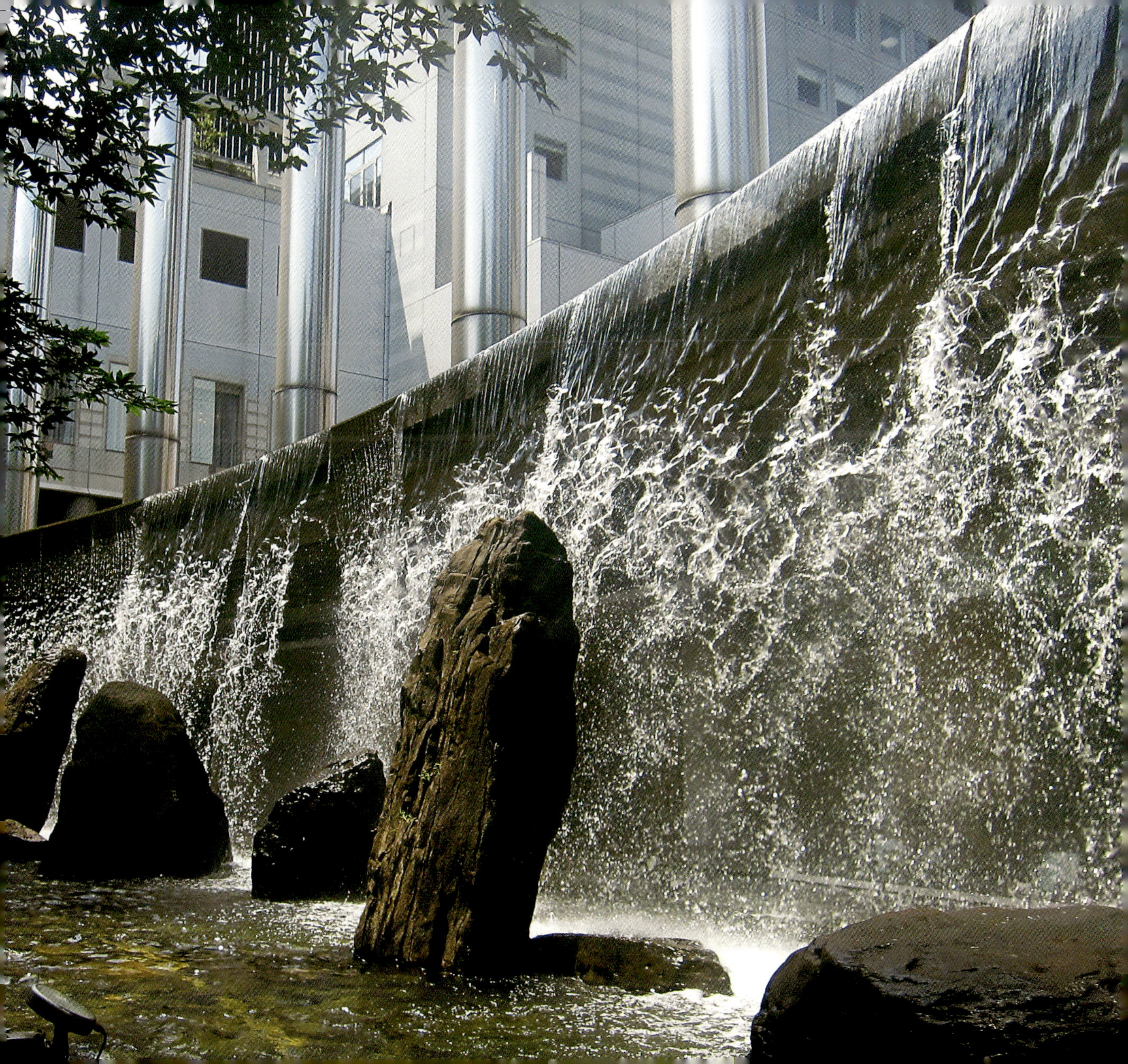

九条の水滝

九本のメタルの列柱から
いっせいに、水がほとばしりでる
九条の水滝
この水は
都市のてっぺんに蓄えられた降雨
メタル、ガラス、コンクリート
の都市を、降雨が清める
清めた水が
地底の九個の岩に
降り注ぐ
九個の岩は
九本の柱から出る
九条の水滝で
いのちを養う

Nine waterfalls

Simultaneously, all the waters gush forth
From nine metallic pillars —
Cascading in full accord
Nine falling waters
These waters — the rainfall that collects
at the top of the city
A metropolis of metal, glass and concrete
Cleansed by the rains
The pure rains —
Pouring down
Onto nine stones planted deep in the earth
Nine waterfalls from nine pillars
Sustaining the life
within these nine stones

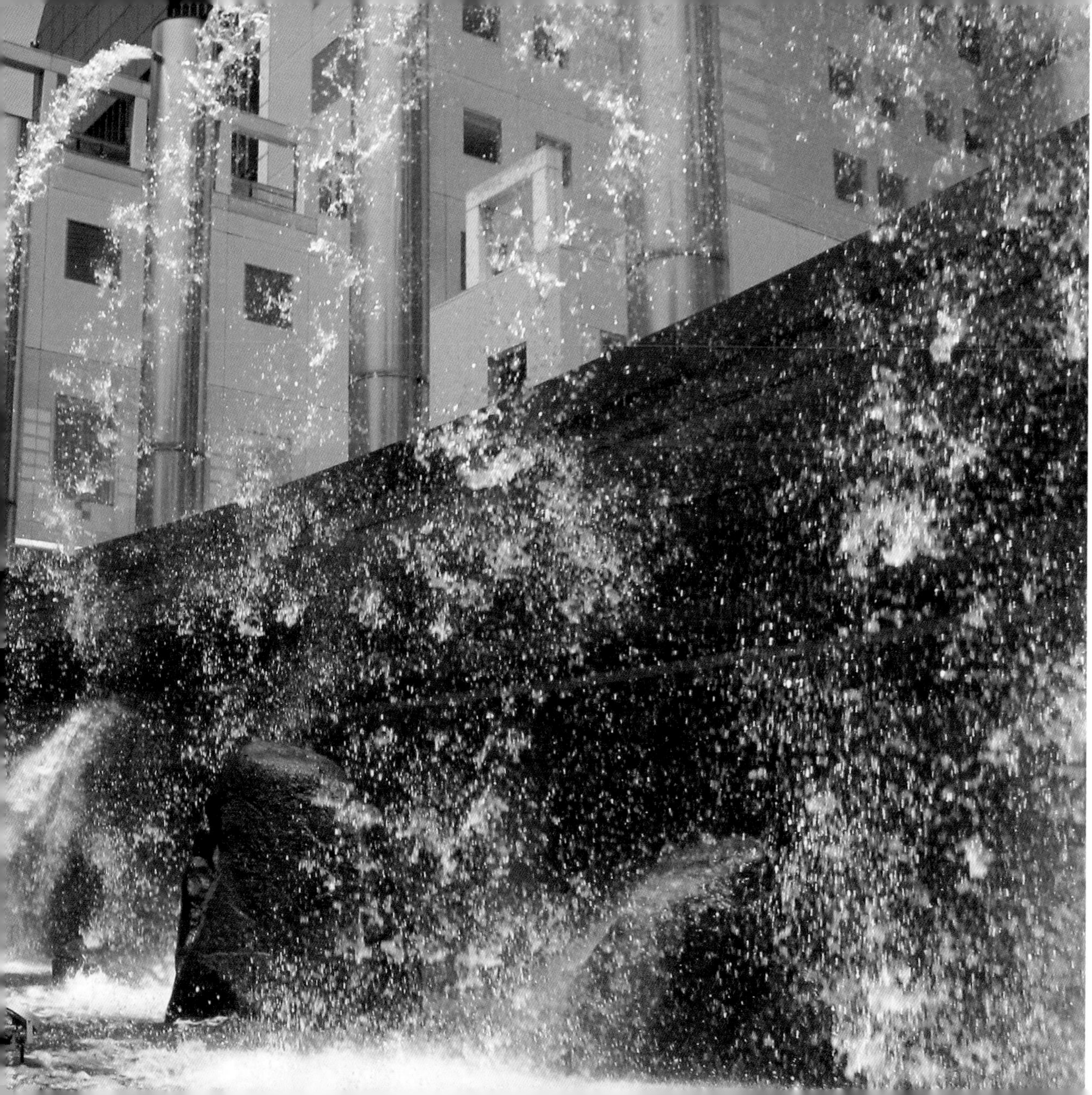

Beyond the cascade

Waterfalls in a mountain valley
Rocks get hidden
What lies behind the falling waters?
And, on the other side of that cascade?
Where I wish to enter —
The dream realized at last
As I view the outside from inside the watery cascade
Water rushes down upon the rocks
The rocks cast off the waters
I gaze from behind the cascading flow
at this harsh encounter between the rocks and falls

滝の向こうから

山岳の谷あいの滝は
岩を隠している
滝の裏になにがあるのだろうか
そして、滝の向こうの世界に、
入りたいと願う
遂にその願いがかなった
水の瀑布の内側から外をみる
岩が水に打たれている
岩が水を跳ね返す
岩と水の厳しい出会いを
水の瀑布の裏から眺めている

石畳の下の饗宴

石畳をめくると、
干潟が現れた
あ！　太古の三葉虫も
顔をのぞかせている
埋立地の街の下は
大海原
わたしたちは、
海の上に生きている

Banquet beneath the pavement

Strip off the concrete cover
A tide pool materializes
Huh? Even the face of an ancient trilobite peeking
Beneath the reclaimed lands —
is the vast ocean
And we —
Living upon this all

Sculptured by
SUGIYAMA Hitoshi

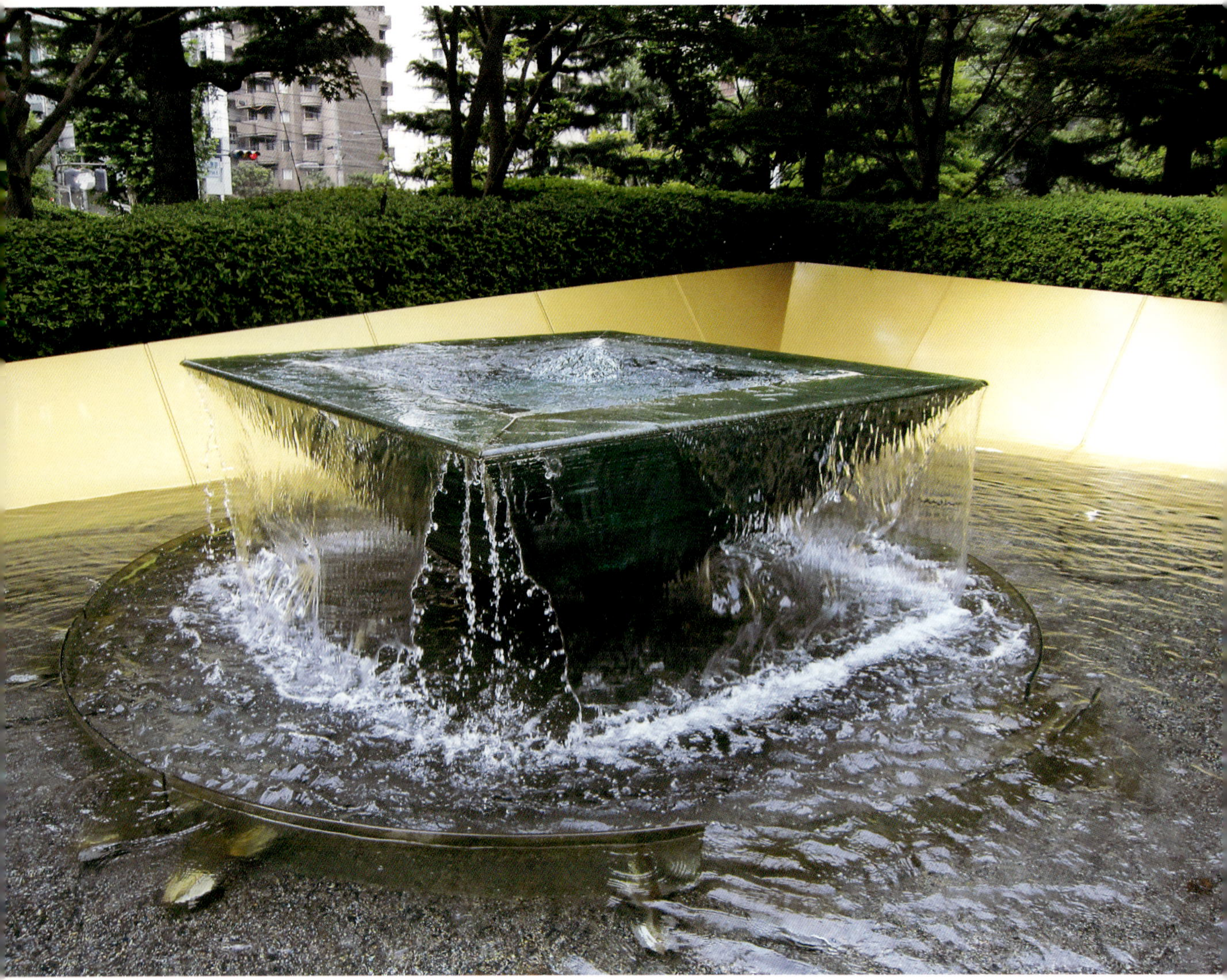

四角・丸・三角

四角が丸に
丸が三角に
三角がもとの四角に
四角・丸・三角
四角・丸・三角が水でつながる
四角い水の水面
四角い水の幕になって落ちる
ざわめく丸い水面
おだやかな三角の水面
そして蒼い空を映している
水はどんな形にも変身する
不思議な生き物だ

Square, circle and triangle

The square becomes the circle
The circle becomes the triangle
The triangle reverts back to the square
Square – circle – triangle
A square water surface
The liaison between these three worlds connected by water
Square – circle – triangle
Transform into a curtain of water, falling
The circular water surface stirs —
Then, the calm triangular water surface —
Is reflected upon the blue sky
Water will adopt any shape
An intriguing life form

逆流の滝

ある日、突然に滝が岩をさかのぼる
水が力を得て、引力に逆らったのだ
輝く太陽、明るさを増す空
地上のぬくもり、土の中の生き物
木々のざわめき
そういったいっさいのうごめきが
水の落下の方向を転換させたのだ
逆流滝は、いのちの増幅現象だ

Reverse waterfall

Suddenly, one day, a waterfall climbs up the rocks
The water gains strength, defying gravity
The sun shines down, the sky intensifies its brightness
In the warmth of the earth, living creatures dwell in the soil
A rustle of the trees
All of this lively squirming
Has caused the falling waters to change direction
The reverse waterfall escalates the phenomenon of life

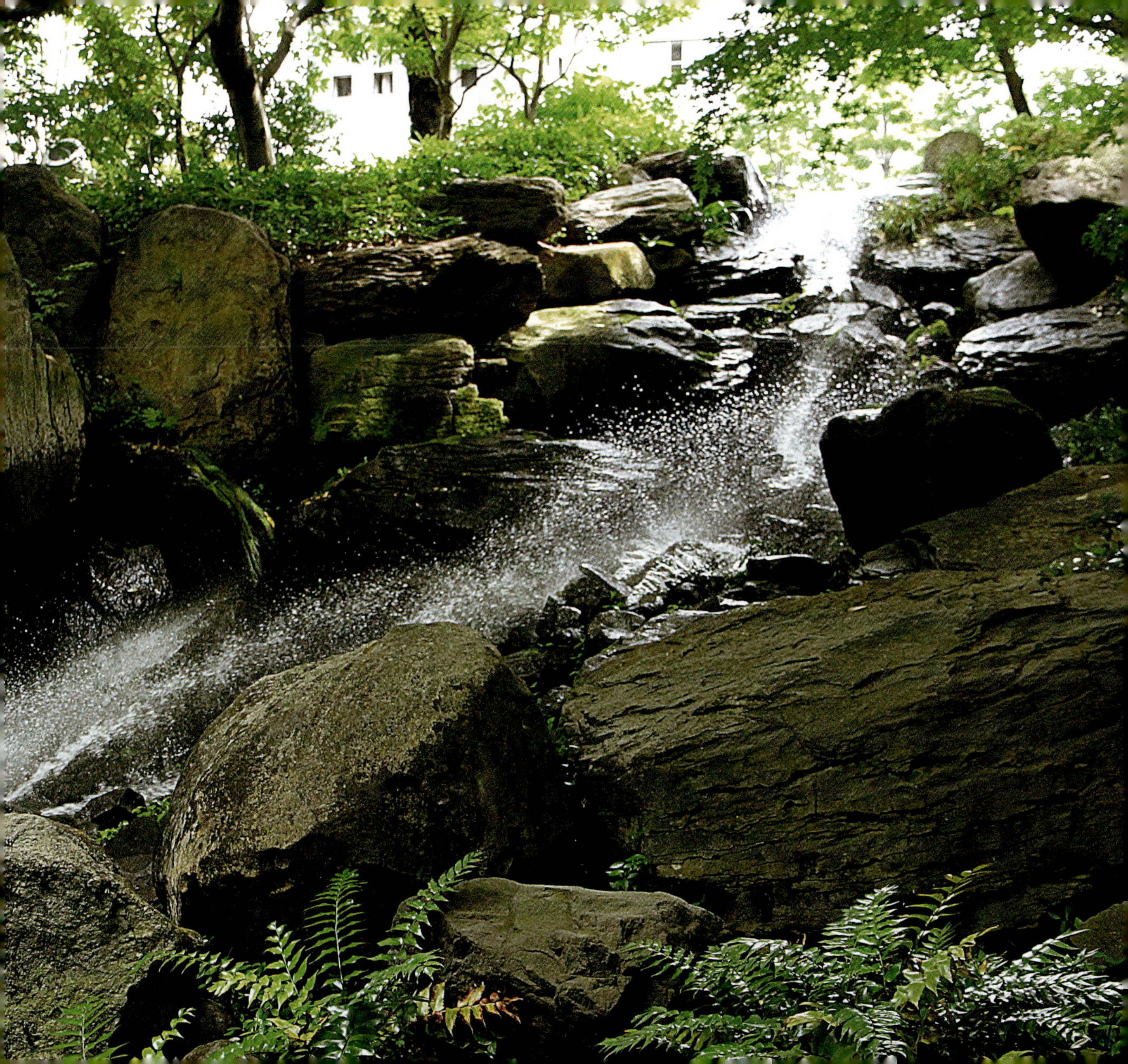

万博記念公園
自然文化園

Natural and Cultural Gardens — Expo'70 Commemorative Park

万博の森

森が蘇った
村の風景の中に、
忽然と現れた
日本万国博覧会場
その跡に、人間がつくった森
時の垢をすいとって、
ここまで蘇った

まわりは、高速道、住宅、
研究所、ホテル、駐車場が
とりかこむ
孤独な森、
ちぢこまりそうな森、
ひとりぼっちな森
あ！　森の外側にも、森を見つけた
お互いに、手をむすびませんか
みどりのむすびめから
入り込んでくる人びと
もう、森は一人ぼっちではない

Expo forest

The forest has been revived,
In a countryside landscape
Suddenly appearing
At the site of Osaka International
Exposition Memorial
A man-made forest on the remains of the Expo
Siphoning off the filth of an era
Regeneration up to this point

Surrounded by highways, residences, institutions,
hotels and parking lots
The solitary forest —
Seems to be shrinking
A lonely forest
But, wait! On the outside of the forest,
lies another forest
Can't we work hand-in-hand?
From green nodes
People enter in
The forest is no longer lonely

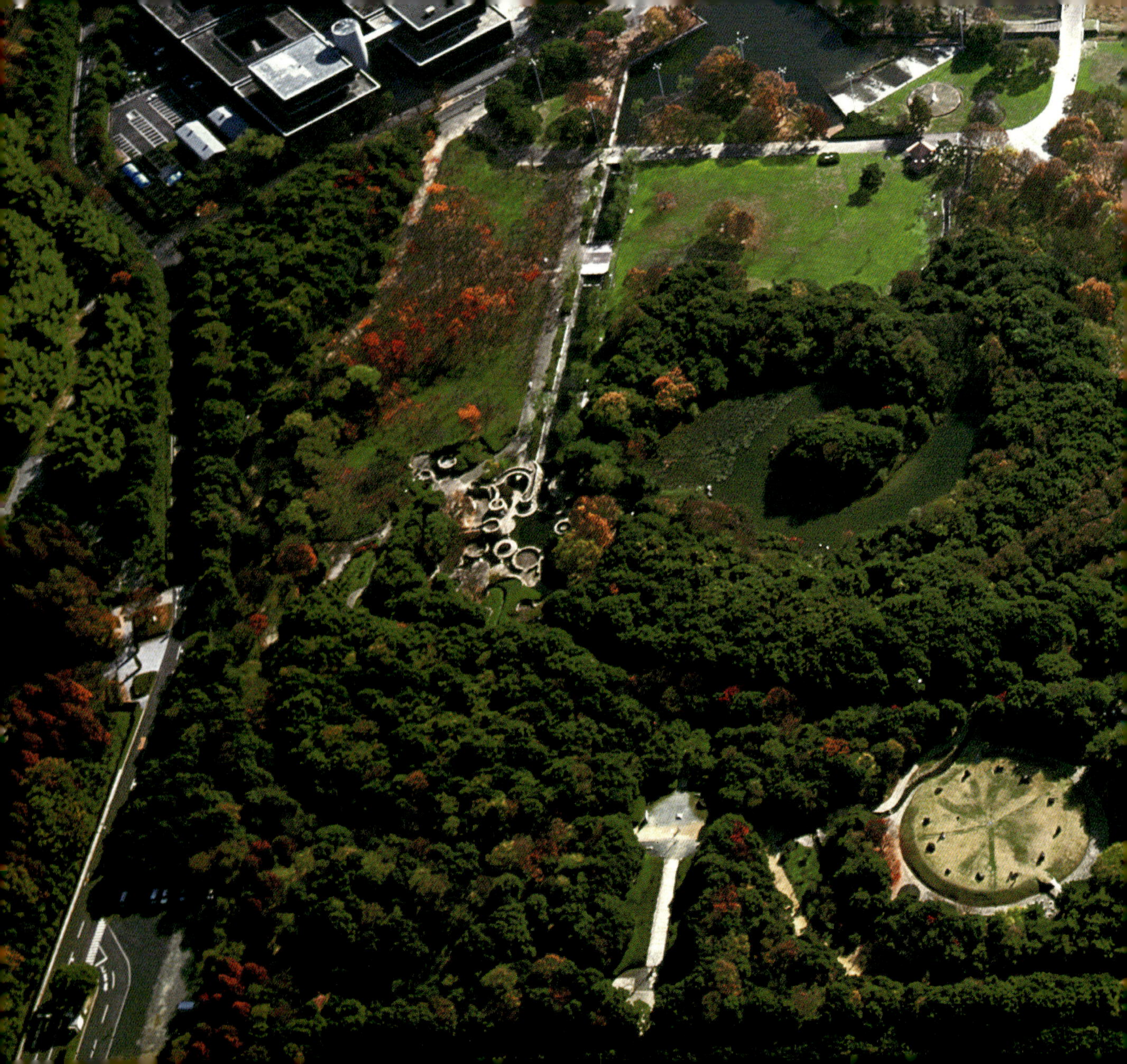

人間がつくった森

人間がつくった森
そこにポッカリあいた二つの穴
一つの森の穴には水面だけ
水鳥だけがあそぶ
人間は入れない
水鳥、昆虫、魚、水草、木々
そよ風が水面をそっとなぜる
うつろいの時が一瞬たちどまる
街のど真ん中の水鳥の楽園
手あかにまみれた自然が
時の彼方に、解き放たれる

Man-made forest

A man-made forest
Two gaping holes there,
One hole is just the water's surface
Only water birds at play there
People are not permitted to enter
Water birds, insects, fish, water plants and trees
A soft breeze gently skims over the surface
The passage of time stops for a moment
A sanctuary for the water birds in the middle of the city
Now smudged with the finger prints of man
Nature is set free in time and space

重なる木々たちの森

木々が重なって、森になる
一直線に刈りこまれた潅木たち
潅木たちの絨毯
その厚ぼったい絨毯を突き破って
薄灰色の巨樹たちが、空にむかって踊る
森のむこうから、同類の巨樹が、
絨毯の上の巨樹たちに問いかける
「なにを、はしゃいでいるのですか」
二つの巨樹の間には
黒々とした森が、うずくまる
薄灰色の巨樹たちが
重なる木々たち

Layered wood

As trees root and layer they become the forest
Neatly pruned shrubs stand in a straight line
A carpet of shrubs
Giant, ash color trees, pierce through this thick carpet
Dancing, as they head into the skies
Beyond these woods, more of the same towering trees
Asking the others on the carpet
"What is all this merrymaking?"
In the space between two giant trees —
A deep and dark wood crouches
Further layers of these giant ash color trees

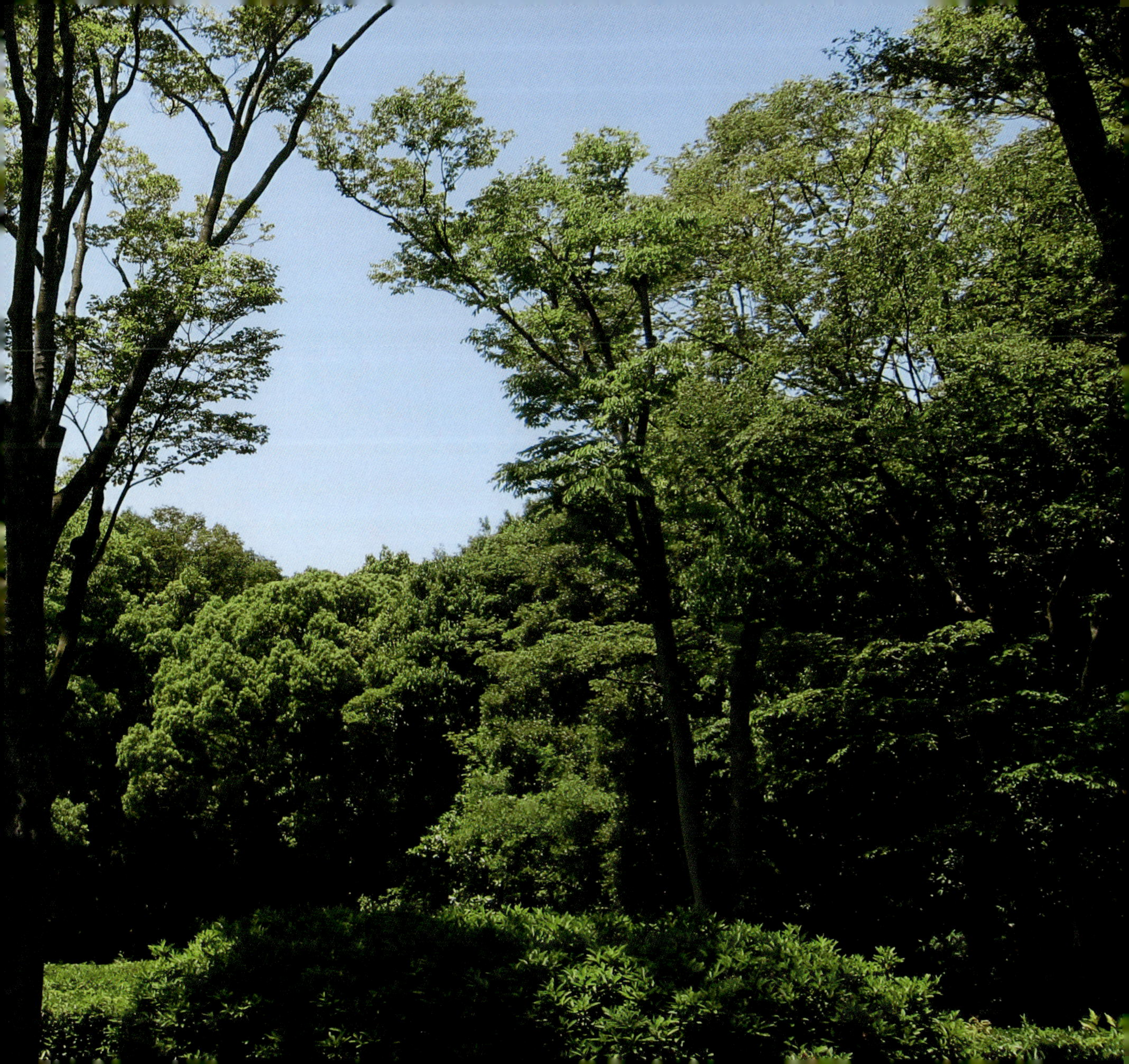

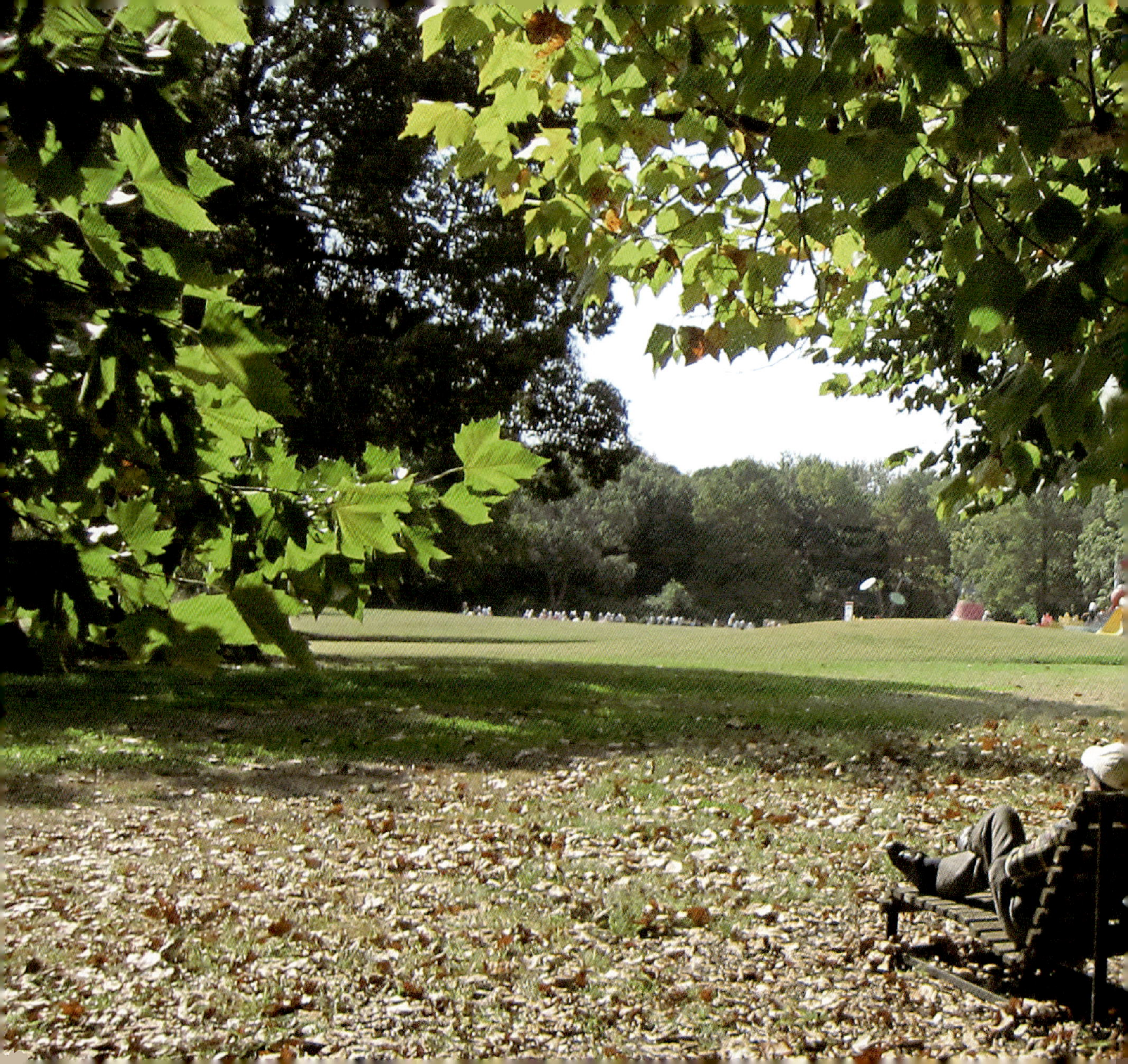

地上十数センチに
浮かぶ長ベンチ

森のなかから
広がる芝生
しめりけの、くらい芝生
そのむこうに、あかるい芝生
子どもたちが飛びはね、
黄色い歓声が飛び交う
その暗と明の変わり目で
地上十数センチに浮かぶ長ベンチが
斜めの彼方をにらんでいる
斜めの長ベンチに横たわる人も
明るい斜めの彼方に
なにかを思いおこそうとしている

Some 10cm off the ground

A long bench floats
From the woods —
Onto a sprawling lawn
Damp and dark, this lawn
And over there, a bright lawn
Where children romp and play
Yellow tinted cries of joyousness
Transitioning between dark and light
A long bench floats, some 10cm off the ground,
Staring intensely beyond the sloping view
People are stretched out on the long, inclined bench —
Also trying to call something to mind
The bright horizon that lies beyond

ススキのあいさつ

しなやかなススキ
風が舞う
ススキがあいさつをする
「元気かい」
「元気だよ」
「少し、寒いかな」
「あっためてあげよう」
ススキのあいさつの真下で
小石たちのおしゃべり
ぺちゃくちゃ、ぺちゃくちゃ
ぺちゃくちゃ、ぺちゃくちゃ
無数のちっちゃな挨拶が
森の中に消えてゆく

Greetings of the *susuki* grass

The suppleness of the *susuki* grass
Whirling in the wind
The *susuki* greets us,
"How are you today?"
"I'm fine."
"It's a bit cold today."
"I can keep you warm."
Beneath this greeting of the *susuki* grass
Pebbles chatter,
"*pecha – kucha, pecha – kucha,*"
"*pecha – kucha, pecha – kucha,*"
So many tiny salutations
Disappearing into the woods

森と人間と水の大蛇

森の中から、水が流れ下る
その水流は、水の大蛇だ
水の大蛇は、森を出てのたうちまわる
あるときは、石ころのはらわたを
あからさまにして、心地よく、眠る
森と水の大蛇は、同床異夢なのか
いや、そこに、人間が引き寄せられる
そうすると
森と人間と水の大蛇が
ひとつになる

Forest, man and water serpent

A waterfall flows downward out of the forest
Undulating, moving like a water serpent
Leaving the forest the water serpent wanders and writhes
One day, guts full of pebbles
Opened up in full view, the serpent now sleeps in comfort
The serpent of water and the wood lives in two separate worlds
But no, people are also pulled into the mix
And thereby —
The forest, man and water serpent
Become one

滝がつたえたいこと

人間がつくった滝
森から噴き出す滝
滝つぼに降り注ぐ飛沫
そのはざまに、人間がいる
滝の鼓動が、
まぢかの人間の胸を叩く、
どんどんどんどんどん
どどどどどどど
滝がつたえたいこと
それは
どんどんどんどんどん
どどどどどどど

Message from the waterfall

Man-made waterfall
Jetting out from the woods
Water collects in a pool at its base
It is in this space that humans exist
The waterfall beats down
Nearby humans beat their chests —
"don – don – don – don – don
do – do – do – do – do – do – do"
This is the message of the waterfall
"don – don – don – don – don
do – do – do – do – do – do – do"

飛び石は、水面に浮いている

水面をあるきたい
水面をあるきたい
水面をあるけないのは
みずかきがないからかな
いや、垂直二足歩行をするからかな
水面をわたりたいのなら
橋があるじゃないか
いや
橋では水面のやわらかさを感じられない
絶妙な解決策があったぞ！
飛び石という素敵な発明品だ
飛び石で、人間は、忍者になる
飛び石で、人間は、水面をあるける
飛び石を歩くとき、足下に注意を！
でも、足下をのぞくと
水面の下に、メダカを見つけた
水面に、大きな空が映っていた

Stepping stones floating on water

I long to walk on water
I yearn to walk on water
Why is it that I can't —
Is it that I haven't got webbed feet?
Or is it that I walk upright on two legs?
If I want to get across the water's surface
Won't I need a bridge?
But —
In using a bridge,
the soft texture of the water's surface can't be felt
I hit upon the perfect solution!
The amazing invention of stepping stones
On stepping stones, humans become ninja
On stepping stones, humans can walk on water
But watch your step on the stones!
And then, just as I look down at my steps —
I find tiny *medaka* fish below the surface
And in the same watery mirror, the vast sky is reflected

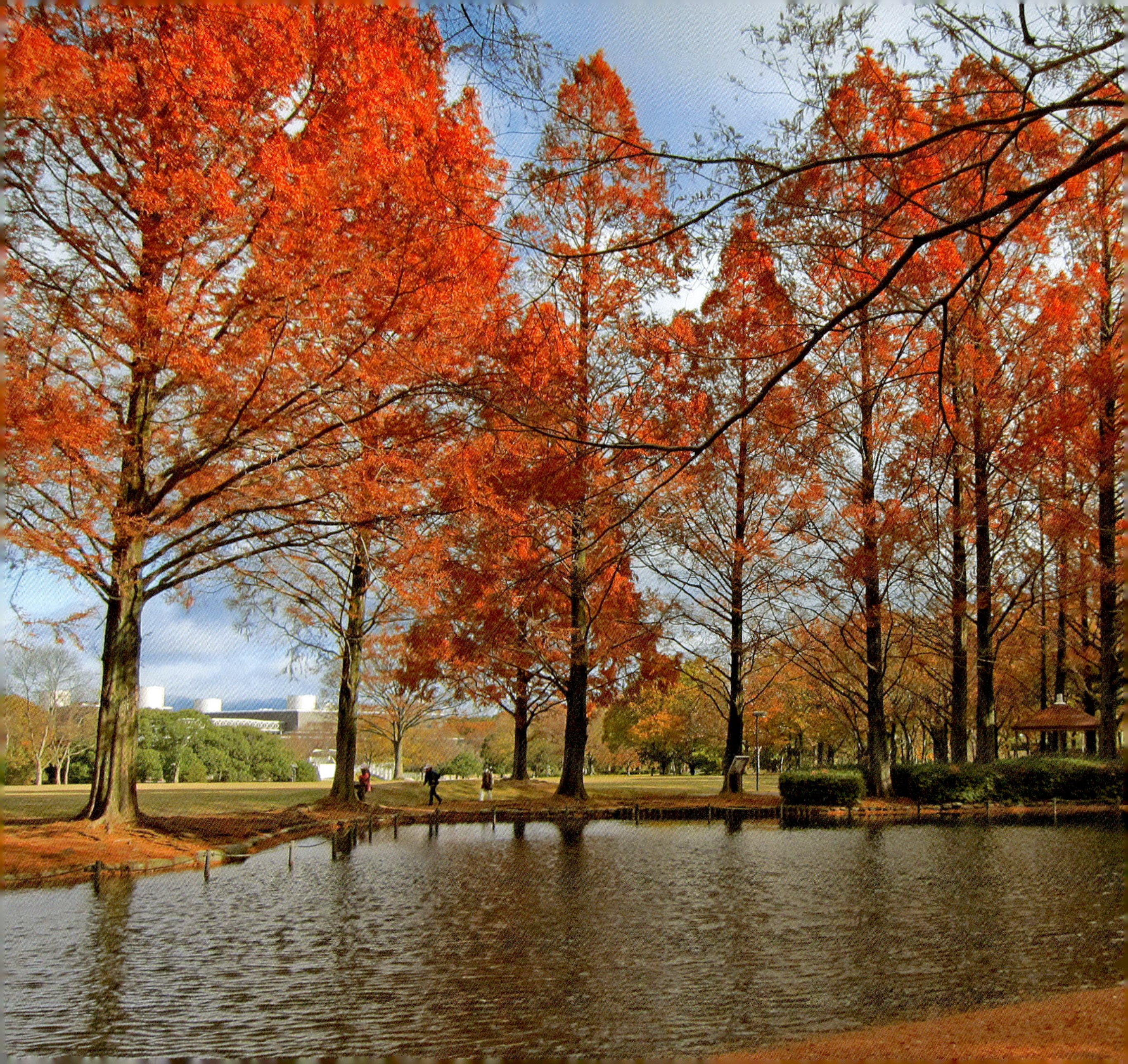

Spanning rust-colored time and space

Dawn redwoods aglow at the water's edge
Turn the water surface a rusty brown
I think back to the dinosaurs —
viewing this landscape two hundred million years ago
Now, spanning time and space
Children in their red caps gather at the bank
One child in red
taps upon the water's surface —
In doing this, the ripples extend to the redwoods on the other side
And shades of red and rust converse,
"Dinosaurs sleep under these waters"

赤褐色の時空を超えて

水辺で燃える
赤褐色のメタセコイアたち
水面が、赤褐色に染まる
この赤褐色の風景を
二億年前の恐竜も
見ていたかもしれない
いま、赤い帽子の子どもたちが
時空を超えて
燃える赤褐色の水辺に集う
赤い服の子どもが
水面をたたく
すると、波紋はむこう岸の
赤褐色のメタセコイアにつたわる
赤と赤褐色が波紋で会話をしている
「水面の下に、恐竜が眠っている」

浅瀬の出会い

湧水、渓流、渓谷、沼、淀み、
淵、瀬、小滝、大滝、
旅をかさねてきた水たちは
ハラッパにでてきて
広河原の浅瀬で小さく踊る
浅瀬の水たちは陽光にさらされる
子どもたちにもさらされる
浅瀬に見え隠れする虫たち
浅瀬が育む小魚たち
浅瀬に眠る貝たち
その浅瀬の水たちが、
子どもたちのくるぶしを
つめたくつつむ

Encounter in shallow waters

Springs, mountain streams, ravines, marshes, backwaters,
Deep pools, streaming currents, waterfalls and cascades
At the end of their long journey,
Traveling waters seem to dance upon the dry river bed
A radiant sun shines on the shallow waters
And shines upon the children too
Small insects peek out of the shallow waters
Tiny fish life grows in the shallow waters
Seashells rest in the shallow waters
And the shallow waters wrap around little ankles
in a cooling swirl

錠前と鍵の風景

錠前型の石のベンチで
身づくろいをする
鍵型に曲がる石畳の道
ざわつく竹やぶを区切る穂の垣根が
やわらかく、静かなひとときを
水路に投げかける
穂の垣根のむこうに万博茶畑が広がる
錠前型と鍵型の風景から
波打つ茶畑の緑の中に、潜り込む
茶の香りで色塗られた建屋で
ひとときの夢をはぐくむ

Lock-and-key landscape

On a stone bench, shaped like a lock
I tidy myself up
A stone footpath bends lock-and-key style
A woven bamboo hedge
clearly demarcates the footpath
from the bamboo grove
A gentle, calming moment drops into the canal
Beyond the hedge, the Expo tea field lies in full view
From this lock-and-key landscape
Moving into the rolling green tea fields
On the gazebo surrounded by the fragrance of tea
A balmy daydream manifests

ふたつがみっつ

森の中のふた筋のまっすぐな帯
地上からみると
プラタナスの巨樹の列
ふたつの帯は
空を切りとる
そこに一直線が現れた
舗石の両側にふたつの水が流れる
ふたつの流れと一直線は、
みっつになって
ビスタの彼方で交わる
ふたつがひとつ
ふたつがみっつ
そして、ひとつになる

Two to three

Two perfectly straight wooded lines
Looking from a ground position
An avenue lined on both sides with plane trees
Two lines cut through the sky
Another straight line appears
The avenue is lined with two shallow streams
Flowing alongside the stone pathway
Two shallow streams, one straight line —
becoming three
All three lines intersect at a point beyond the vista
Two into one
Two into three
And finally, all one

森の空中回廊で、子どもたちは猿になる

梢に鳥たちの巣がある
梢に葉っぱが色づく
梢に紫色の実がなる
梢をそよ風がゆらす
梢を淡い雨がぬらす
梢に白い雪が化粧をほどこす
木登りをしても梢まで近づけることができない
その梢たちに、そっと近づける
それが、森の空中回廊だ
梢から梢へ、森の空中散歩
子どもたちは、梢に囲まれて、猿になる

Children become monkeys on the sky walk in the canopy

In the treetops, nests for birds
In the treetops, the changing colors of autumn leaves
In the treetops, yielding fruits of deep purple
In the treetops, gentle breezes blowing
In the treetops, dampened by light rain showers
White snow, applied like powder on the face
to dress up the high branches
We cannot approach the treetops by climbing,
We approach gently
This is the sky walk in the canopy
Inching closer, treetop by treetop
Children surrounded by the forest,
Become monkeys

森の空中回廊で、子どもたちは鳥になる

万博の森で、子どもたちは鳥になれる
森の中には万博のパビリオンが眠る
万博の森から顔を出す「森の回廊」で
子どもたちは、森の底から
吹きあげてきた風に、両手を広げる
すると、子どもたちは、森の上を飛べる
森の回廊は、うねうねと
森の中をさまよう
そのむこうに
昔のお祭り広場を見つめていた
太陽の塔がある
その太陽の塔は、
いま、森に包まれている
子どもたちは、記憶の万博、
森の中に埋もれたパビリオン、
森の上をつないで
太陽の光を浴びて、
鳥になる

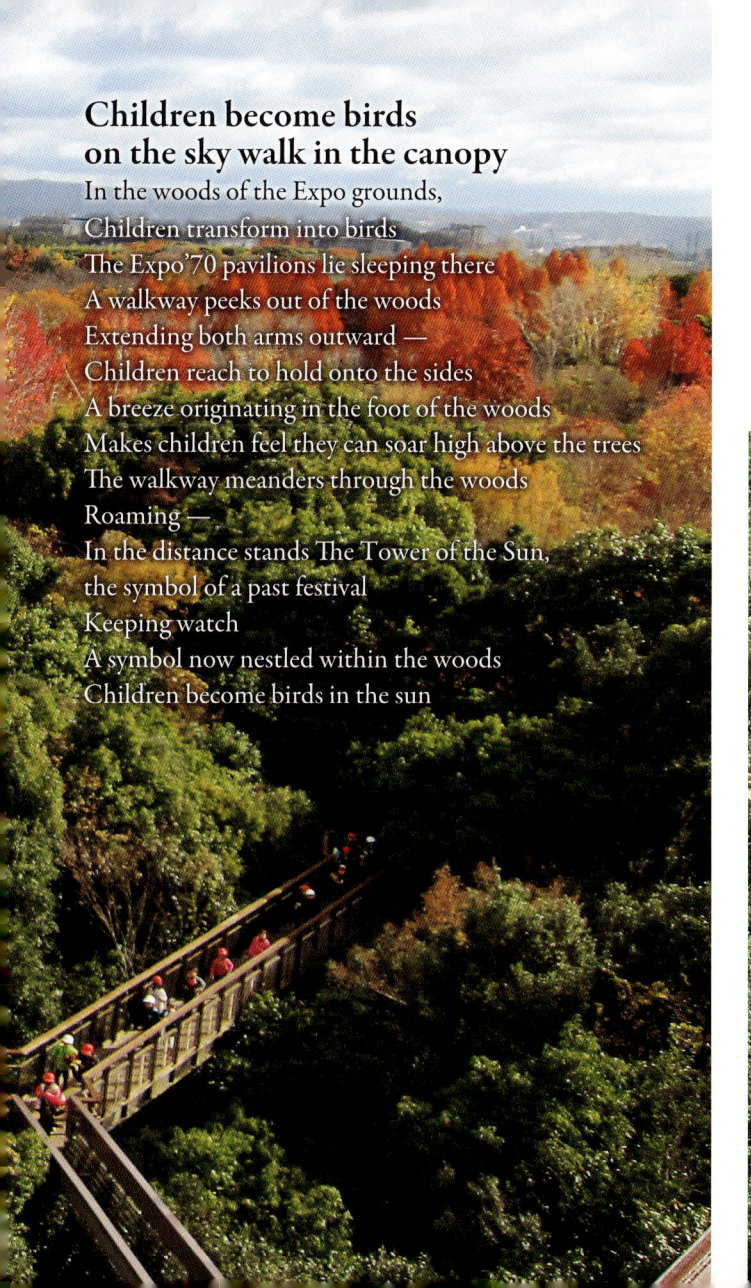

Children become birds
on the sky walk in the canopy

In the woods of the Expo grounds,
Children transform into birds
The Expo'70 pavilions lie sleeping there
A walkway peeks out of the woods
Extending both arms outward —
Children reach to hold onto the sides
A breeze originating in the foot of the woods
Makes children feel they can soar high above the trees
The walkway meanders through the woods
Roaming —
In the distance stands The Tower of the Sun,
the symbol of a past festival
Keeping watch
A symbol now nestled within the woods
Children become birds in the sun

白鳥庭園（名古屋市熱田区 約4ヘクタール）
基本設計・実施設計 吉村元男＋㈱環境事業計画研究所
工事監修 川崎幸次郎

Shirotori Garden (Nagoya City • 4 hectares)
Master plan and design: YOSHIMURA Motoo + Environmental Development Institute
Director: KAWASAKI Koujiro

コンセプト

御嶽山を源流とする木曽川など三川がつくる広大な濃尾平野を舞台に築かれた名古屋市民のアイデンティティを風景として凝縮している。御嶽山の源流、渓谷、渓流、分流、熱田の港、海洋の風景を回遊式庭園として構成したのが白鳥庭園。

汐入の庭

埋めたてが進むまでの、この地域は海岸線に近く、潮の満ち干が見られた。その記憶を呼び起こそうと、「汐入の庭」を設計した。海岸の風景は、潮の満ち干で一変する。自然の営みを感じる風景がある。

空から見た白鳥庭園の汐入の庭と清羽亭

庭園周辺

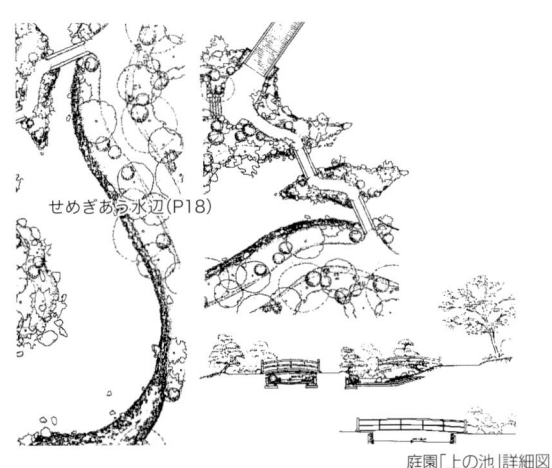

庭園「上の池」詳細図

白鳥庭園全体平面図

汐入の庭に込められた宇宙（P22）

せめぎあう水辺（P18）

遊濱亭

上の池

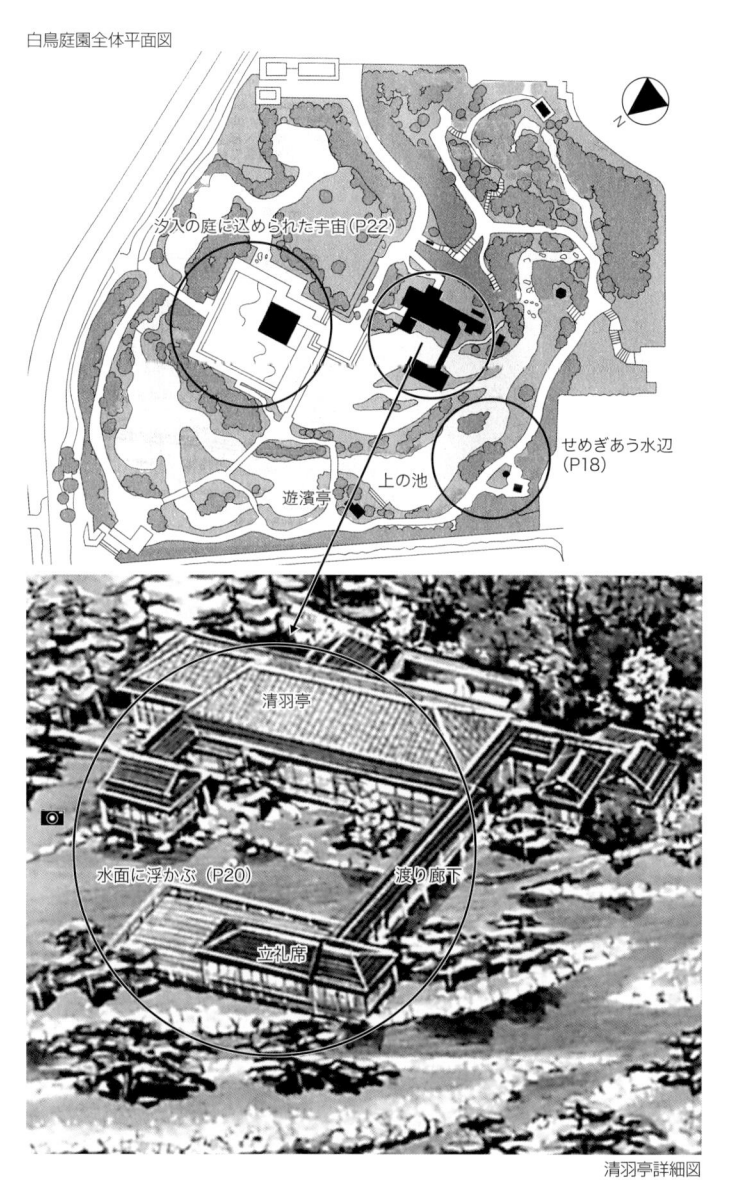

清羽亭

水面に浮かぶ（P20）

渡り廊下

立礼席

清羽亭詳細図

上／立礼席
中／立礼席への渡り廊下
下／立礼席から一の間・二の間を望む

清羽亭

基本設計 吉村元男＋㈱環境事業計画研究所
実施設計 ㈶京都伝統建築技術協会（監修 中村昌生）
茶会のできる本館と、香道、句会、管弦、コンサートなどの催しができる施設。主屋と二棟の茶室と州浜に浮かぶ立礼席茶室からなる。全体は、水辺に降り立つ白鳥が羽を休めているイメージにした。

大阪府立国際会議場 葦原の庭（大阪市北区 約0.3ヘクタール）
設計 吉村元男＋㈱環境事業計画研究所
建築設計 ㈱黒川紀章建築都市設計事務所

Garden of Reeds — Osaka International Conference Center (Osaka City • 0.3 hectares)
Design: YOSHIMURA Motoo + Environmental Development Institute
Architecture Design: KUROKAWA Kisho Architect & Associates

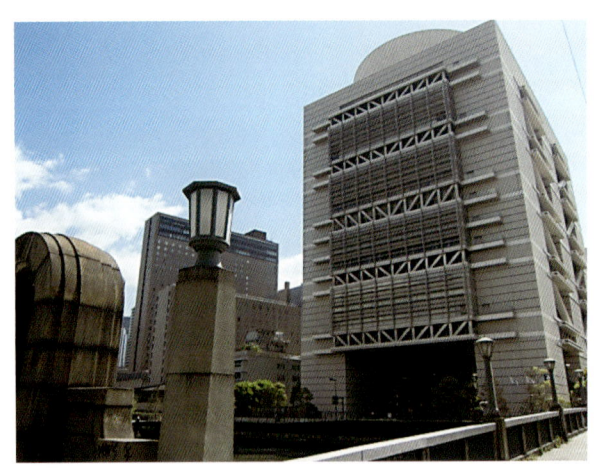

正面から見た国際会議場

葦原の庭と特別会議場
大阪国際会議場の最上階に設けられた「葦原の庭」。特別会議場での緊張した会議の合間の休息時に鑑賞する庭園。大阪の原風景である葦原を表現している。(平面図とイメージ図は、基本設計時のもの)

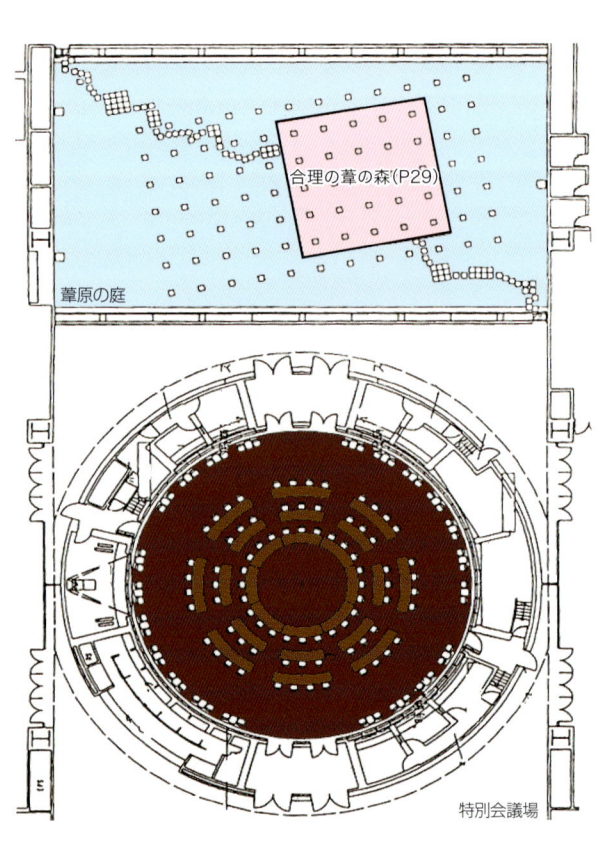

葦原の庭　特別会議場

葦原の庭と特別会議場平面図

76

葦原の庭

葦原を想起させる列柱によって、水の都大阪の原風景を抽象的に創りだした。葦原が水面から勢いよく伸びるように群棲する姿を、大阪の力として表現。水面のつくる水鏡は葦原と天を写し、葦原と人びとを天空に浮遊するかの世界に誘う。

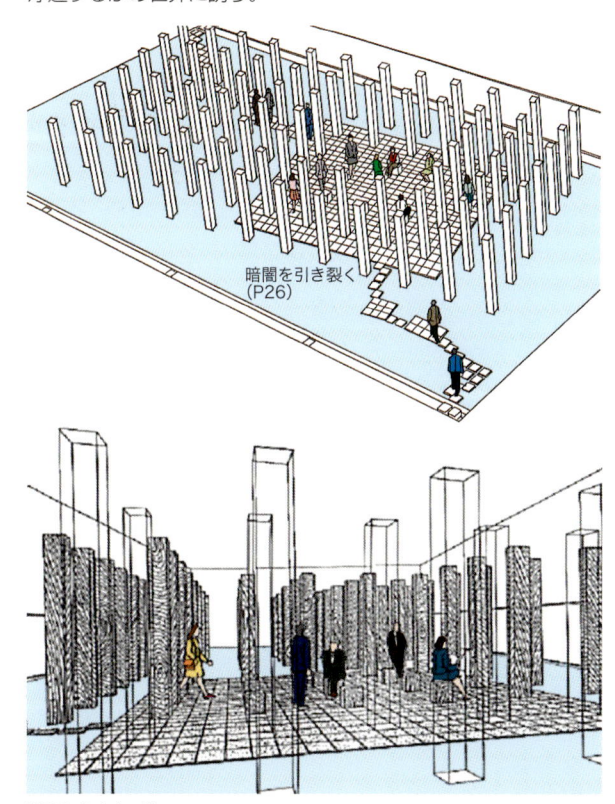

葦原の庭イメージ

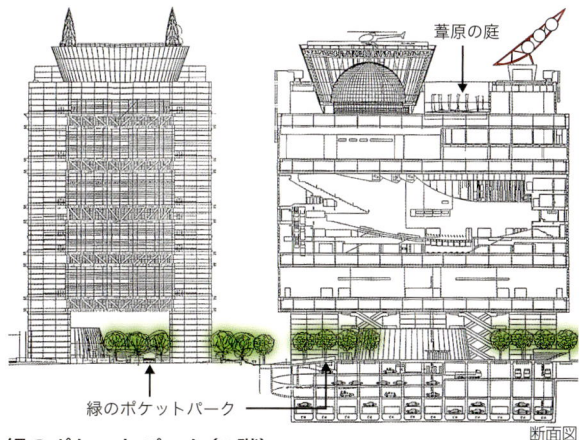

断面図

緑のポケットパーク（1階）

建物の1階の広々とした地上レベルの開放的な吹き抜け空間に、樹林によるポケットパークとして、憩いの交流広場を設計。

新梅田シティ 中自然の森・公園緑地（大阪市北区 約4ヘクタール）
設計 吉村元男＋㈱環境事業計画研究所
建築設計 原 広司＋アトリエファイ建築研究所

A mid-wild Forest & Green Park — New Umeda City (Osaka City • 4 hectares)
Design: YOSHIMURA Motoo + Environmental Development Institute
Architecture Design: HARA Hiroshi + Atelier Phi

新梅田シテイの中を、水が循環する

空からの雨水は、新梅田シティの超高層ビルを清め、貯留される。やがて、その水は「水の惑星」を表象する「都市に、抱かれた地球」に九本の列柱滝から注がれる。滝は九個の岩を叩きつけ、その水は渓谷・渓流を抜け、沼、逆流の滝（P44）、地中へと導かれ、大海に至る。地中の滝は、再び地表に湧きだす。四角、丸、三角の噴水（P43）と渦巻き噴水だ。渦巻き噴水の水はさらに北上し、キャナル（水路）となって花渦に吸い込まれ、再び花渦で湧水となる。湧水は花野を潤して空中庭園の真下の広場を横切り、幅40ｍの大滝（P34）になって「抱かれた地球」（P32）に注がれる。

だれでもいつでも散策できる公開空地

最上階の空中庭園によって連結された二棟の超高層建築とホテル、事務所棟からなる建築群の地上の大半は、公開空地として散策、休息、屋外イベントなどに開放されている。その中に中自然の森、花野里山、キャナル散策路等がある。

新梅田シティの公園緑地全体図

四角・丸・三角(P43)
ウェスティンホテル
抱かれた地球(P32)
石畳の下の饗宴(P40)

花渦
シティを循環した水が吸い込まれる

石畳の下の饗宴(P40)
キャナル散策路

キャナル(水路)
石畳の下の干潟水がとうとう流れている

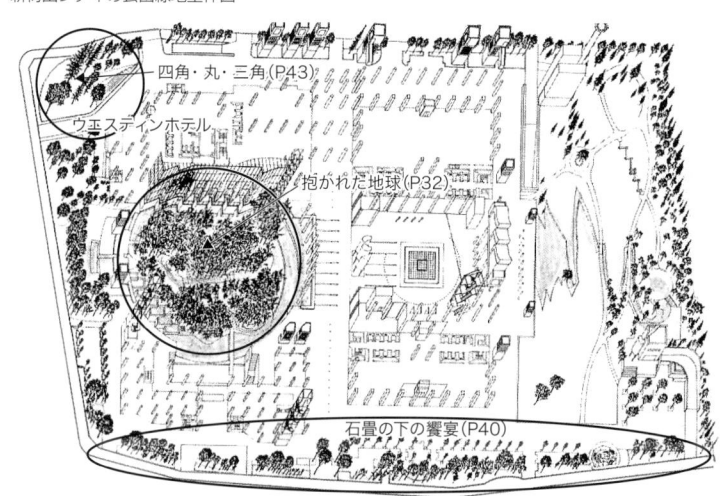

空中庭園
中自然の森

空から望む梅田スカイビル

キャナル散策路と水の循環

新梅田シティの東に設けられた散策路。渦巻き噴水から水が噴き出し、キャナルをとおって、花渦庭園で地中に吸い込まれる。

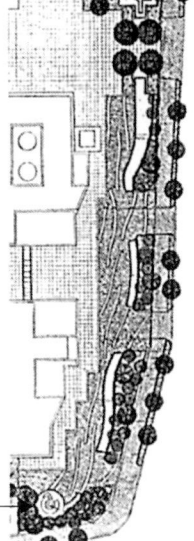

渦巻き噴水
地中からの水が噴き出す

79

万博記念公園自然文化園（吹田市、豊中市 約100ヘクタール）
基本設計・実施設計 吉村元男＋㈱環境事業計画研究所
Natural and Cultural Gardens — Expo'70 Commemorative Park (Osaka • 100 hectares)
Master plan and design: YOSHIMURA Motoo + Environmental Development Institute

破壊から自然の再生へ　里山→ EXPO'70 →裸地→万博記念公園

1　万博開催前の里山と田園風景

3　パビリオン撤去・裸地（1971年）

2　日本万国博覧会（1970年）

4　森が蘇った14年後（1985年）

三つの「み」計画

みどり（森）・みち・みずの組みあわせで、多様な自然と風景を創造

閉じられた森

閉じられた森（緑）の中を道が走る

開かれた森

閉じられた森に空地を設ける。森の中に陽だまりができる

開かれた森（緑）の中を道が走る。開放感のある広場が、森の中に生まれる

溢れ（水）があると、動きが生まれる

水が流れ、躍動感が付け加わる

水面をつくると、静けさが生みだされる

水面をつくることで、大きな自然を演出できる

万博の森──100年再生計画

30周年は森再生の第一段階。目標を100年後の2070年に設定し、巨樹の森、多様な森の形成にむけて管理されている。

100年再生計画				2070年以降
再生前期 1971〜2001 植栽 再生 実績評価	再生中期 2001〜31 若返り間伐	再生終期 2031〜70 若返り間伐	再生百周年記念事業	巨樹・巨木の森 自立する森 野生の森 生物多様性の森

万博の森への生物導入計画

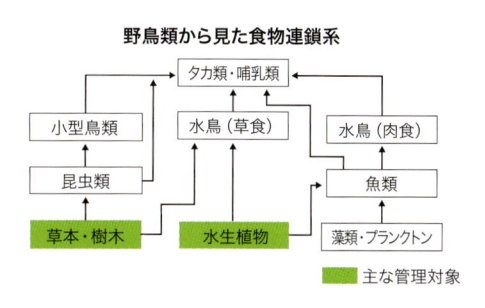

再生された森に、多様な生態系を創りたい。そのために、起伏に富んだ地形と、多様な植栽樹種、水辺が設計された。多様な生態系の基礎は、食物連鎖系の確立。現在は、すでに食物連鎖系の上位のタカが生息するまでになり、生態系がよみがえっていることが確認されている。

野鳥類から見た食物連鎖系

森の再生設計

自然の多様な森を一から再生するには、多くの年月がかかる。さまざまな形状と大きさの樹種の樹木を、互いが邪魔せずに成長させる初期植樹をした。そのうえで、年月の経過でそれぞれの樹種の生育プログラムを念頭においた成長管理をしている。30年前後を経過した頃から、密生した森の若返り間伐を行なっている。

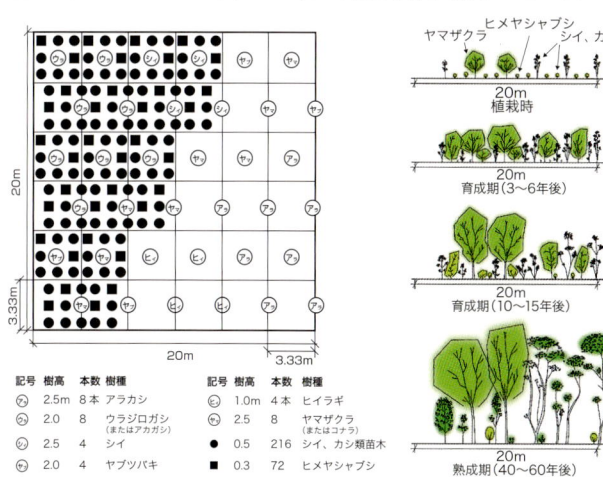

植栽後5〜10年経過の森（1975年頃）

パビリオンが撤去された跡に植樹した当時の西の丘からの風景。お祭り広場の大屋根（丹下健三氏設計、その後に撤去）と大屋根を突き抜けるようにそびえたつ太陽の塔（岡本太郎氏設計）がみえる。

自然文化園

パビリオンが建設されていた100ヘクタールの跡地に、裸地から森を再生した。植栽は1971年に始まり、40年を超えて豊かな自然がよみがえっている。80万本の多様な樹木が植栽された。

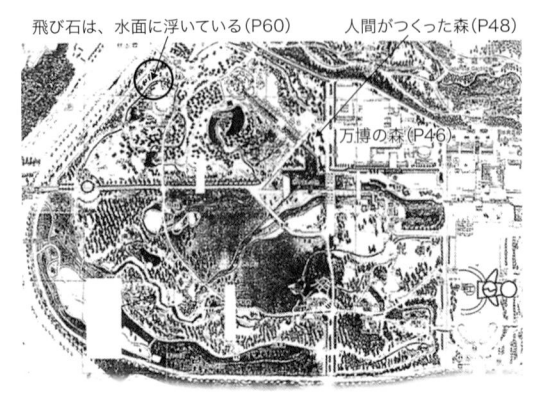

飛び石は、水面に浮いている(P60)　人間がつくった森(P48)
万博の森(P46)

森と人間と水の大蛇(P56)
飛び石は、水面に浮いている(P60)
人間がつくった森(P48)
日本庭園
ふたつがみっつ(P68)
浅瀬の出会い(P64)
ススキのあいさつ(P54)
錠前と鍵の風景(P66)
赤褐色の時空を超えて(P63)　重なる木々たちの森(P50)

植栽のための盛土と土壌づくり

パビリオンが撤去された地盤に盛り土を施し、公園の造成地には植栽土壌を加え、植栽した。

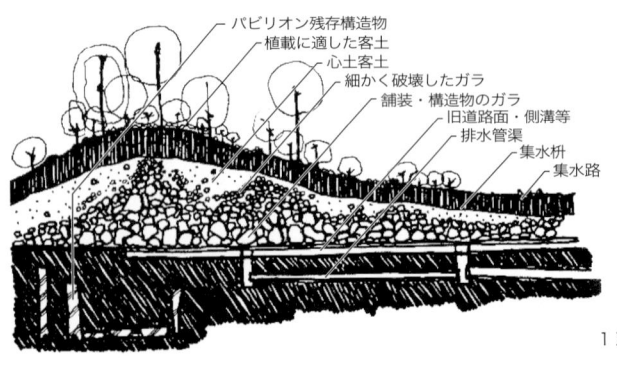

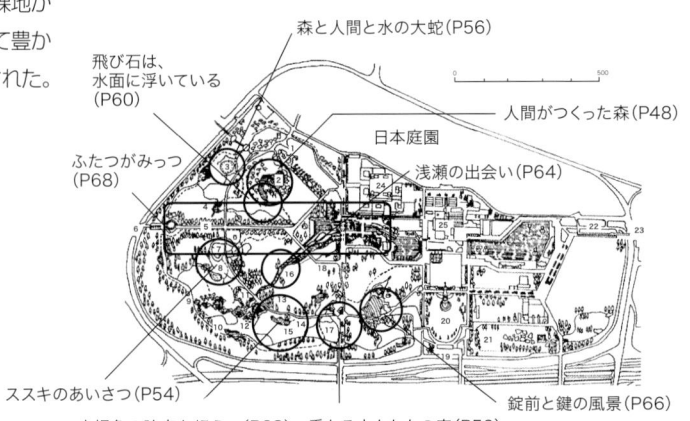

パビリオン残存構造物
植栽に適した客土
心土客土
細かく破壊したガラ
舗装・構造物のガラ
旧道路面・側溝等
排水管渠
集水枡
集水路

水の流れと池と沼

森を早く成長させるために、森の中を水が縦横にめぐるように流れ・池・沼を配した。水面からあがる水蒸気が森に湿り気を与え、森をよみがえらせることに成功した。水はさらに多くの生物を呼び戻し、またさまざまな景観をつくって、ここを訪れる人たちにうるおいと安らぎの場所を提供している。

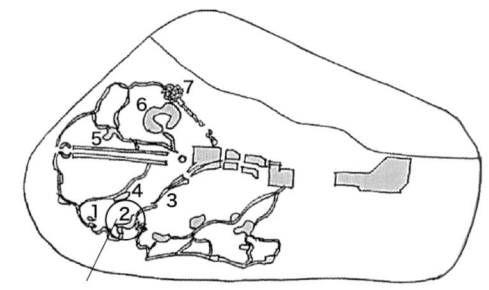

滝がつたえたいこと(P58)
1 双子池、2 大滝、3 河原、4 しょうぶ池、5 ひょうたん池、6 水鳥の池、7 春の泉

森の配置図

密生林・疎生林・散開林の三つの異なるタイプの森を、相互に入り乱れるように配置し、多様な自然の回復と豊かな風景の創造を意図した。

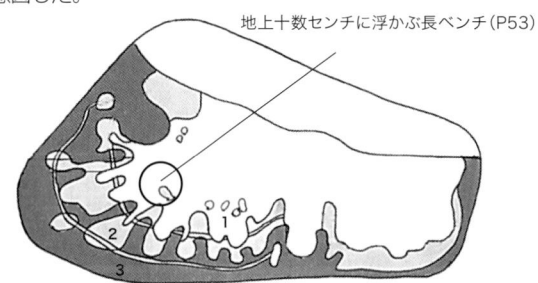

地上十数センチに浮かぶ長ベンチ (P53)

森のタイプ (1 散開林、2 疎生林、3 密生林)

森のタイプ

特性項目 \ 樹木型	密生林	疎生林	散開林
特性	自然の再現 (自立した森) を目指した常緑樹を中心とした樹林であると同時に外部の様々な悪影響 (騒音、排ガス、強風など) を遮断する重要な役割も果たしている	落葉樹を中心とした比較的明るい樹林。魅力あるスポットを配し、景観の変化を楽しむ	芝生を中心とした明るく広々とした空間
樹林被度	70〜100%	50〜80%	10〜20%
林床	きわめて少ない	ササ、ススキ、野草	芝生
潅木	耐陰性樹種	二次林の構成種	低い刈込
利用度	低	中	高
行動の自由度	小	中	大
主な利用内容	散策、自然観察	休養、散策、鑑賞、自然観察	休養、鑑賞、ピクニック、軽いスポーツ
保育管理	自然の生態系による	下刈り、落葉還元、間伐	刈込、施肥、灌水
主要樹種	シイ、カシ、クス、シロダモ、ツバキ等	クヌギ、アベマキ、コナラ、ナラガシワ等	ムク、エノキ、クス、カシ、シイ等
計画面積	80ha (外周部保存緑地約40haを含む)	35ha	10ha
イメージ			

森の回廊「ソラード」
基本設計・実施設計 吉村元男＋㈱環境事業計画研究所

Sky walk in the canopy, "SORADO"
Master plan and design: YOSHIMURA Motoo + Environmental Development Institute

自然文化園・森の回廊

万博30周年記念事業として、森をサルや鳥の目線から観察できる二つの展望台と「ソラード」と名づけられた長さ300メートルの「森の回廊」を設計。さまざまなタイプの樹林をめぐり、地上とは異なる森の姿を体感できる。(下平面図と立面図は、基本設計時のもの)

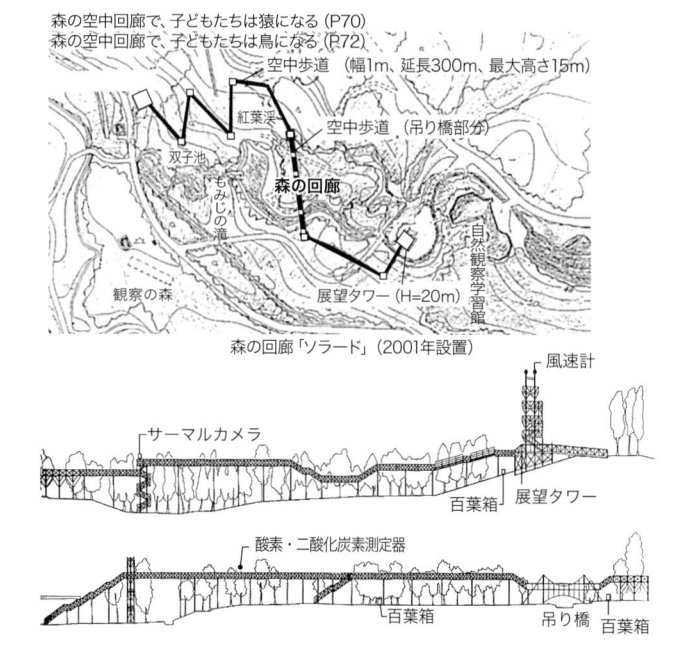

森の空中回廊で、子どもたちは猿になる (P70)
森の空中回廊で、子どもたちは鳥になる (P72)

空中歩道 (幅1m、延長300m、最大高さ15m)
紅葉渓
空中歩道 (吊り橋部分)
双子池
もみじの滝
森の回廊
自然観察学習館
観察の森
展望タワー (H=20m)

森の回廊「ソラード」(2001年設置)

風速計
サーマルカメラ
百葉箱
展望タワー
酸素・二酸化炭素測定器
百葉箱
吊り橋
百葉箱

著者の略歴
風景造園家　吉村元男　よしむら・もとお／Landscape Architect YOSHIMURA Motoo

1937年、京都市に生まれる。京都大学農学部林学科造園学専攻卒業。
㈱環境事業計画研究所所長、鳥取環境大学教授をへて、現在、㈱環境事業計画研究所会長、地球ネットワーク会議代表。この間、奈良女子大学、大阪大学、京都工芸繊維大学、鳥取大学などで非常勤講師を歴任。作品に、「万博記念公園の基本設計・実施設計」（日本造園学会賞）、「鎮守の森の保存修景研究」（環境省環境優良賞共同）、「新梅田シティ」（大阪府都市景観最優秀賞、建設省都市景観大賞共同）、「白鳥公園」（名古屋市景観賞）、「都市公園での功労」（北村徳太郎賞）などがある。著書に、『空間の生態学』、『都市に生きる方途──応用生態学の構想』、『吉村元男作品集』、『都市は野生でよみがえる──花と緑の都市戦略』、『エコハビタ環境創造の都市──環境創造の都市』、『地域発・ゼロエミッション──廃棄物ゼロの循環型まちづくり』、『森が都市を変える──野生のランドスケープデザイン』、『ランドスケープデザイン──野生のコスモロジーと共生する風景の創造』、『水辺の計画と設計』、『風景のコスモロジー』、『地域油田──環節都市が開く未来』などがある。

写真撮影・提供にご協力いただいた方がた
株式会社メイセイ出版、株式会社プロセスアーキテクチュア、名古屋市、積水ハウス株式会社、独立行政法人日本万国博覧会記念機構、廣田治雄氏

翻訳 translation
吉村弘子 YOSHIMURA Hiroko、モーラ・ハーリー Maura HURLEY

〈シリーズ　人と風と景と〉
吉村元男の「景」と「いのちの詩」

吉村元男 著

2013年7月10日発行
発行所◎京都通信社
　　　京都市中京区室町通御池上る御池之町 309 番地
　　　〒604-0022
　　　電話 075-211-2340
　　　http://www.kyoto-info.com/
発行者◎中村基衞
装　丁◎中曽根孝善
製　版◎豊和写真製版株式会社
印　刷◎土山印刷株式会社
製　本◎株式会社吉田三誠堂製本所

Seen Scenes Series
Landscape and the Poetry of Life

Written by: YOSHIMURA Motoo
Published by: Kyoto Tsushinsha Press
　　　　　　　309 Oike-no-cho Nakagyo-ku Kyoto 604-0022
　　　　　　　http://www.kyoto-info.com/
Designed by: NAKASONE Takayoshi
First published: July 2013

©2013　京都通信社
Printed in Japan　ISBN978-4-903473-71-0

シリーズ「人と風と景と」発行の趣旨
景はともかく、風は捉えどころがない。頬にあたってようやく、あるいは木の葉を揺らし、煙をたなびかせて、はじめてその存在を感じる。透き通っていて、向こうのものを遮ったり邪魔したりすることもない。自在に形を変えて、なにかあればスルリと抜け逃げる。それが風流や風情というものだろう。とはいえ、これを欠くとたいていのものは窒息する。なんとも面倒な存在だ。しかも、そういう風と景には、人の意志や意思が介在している。日本の自然は野生ではない。そんな人の働きかけや感性に温かい視線を送ってみようというのが、このシリーズである。　　京都通信社を代表して　中村基衞

＊お近くの書店にないばあいは、弊社ホームページから直接ご注文ください。
　お電話でのご注文には即日発送いたします。